Building Wealth in Your 20s
A Step by Step Guide

by David Brewster

Formatted, Converted, and Distributed by eBookIt.com
http://www.eBookIt.com

ISBN-13: 9781456642075 (paperback)
ISBN-13: 9781456642068 (ebook)
ISBN-13: 9781456642082 (audiobook)

Dear Esteemed Reader,

Thank you immensely for choosing this book to join your collection. We imagine that you've already embarked on an exploration of ideas within these pages, and we couldn't be happier about it!

Now, if you find yourself chuckling, pondering, or even debating with the words in front of you, we'd absolutely love to hear about it. If you can spare a few moments to pen down your thoughts in a review, we would be as delighted as a dictionary on a spelling bee!

An Amazon review would be excellent - but hey, we're far from picky. Whether it's a scribble on the back of a grocery list, a tweet, or even a message in a bottle (though that might take a while to reach us), your feedback is gold.

Writing a review might not be as fun as a spontaneous dance-off, but we promise it'll bring grins to our faces, warmth to our hearts, and incredibly valuable insights to future readers.

With Gratitude,

Bo Bennett, PhD
Publisher
Archieboy Holdings, LLC.

Table of Contents

Introduction

Money, cash, dough, green - whatever you call it, it's the world's ticket to just about everything. But the game isn't about who has the most down the road; it's about who can play smart right now. You're in your 20s, and while that might seem early to worry about finances, it's exactly the right time to start. We're not talking about stashing away every penny and living like a hermit. We're talking about understanding money, wealth, and the art of saving so that you can live freely without the weight of financial stress.

One of the biggest roadblocks on the way to financial freedom is a psychological barrier - a mental block that prevents many people from saving effectively. Do you find yourself thinking, "I'll start saving once I'm making more," or "I'm young, there's plenty of time"? These might sound like valid arguments in your head, but they are, in fact, delaying tactics your mind uses to postpone action. This book will help you shatter these misconceptions and equip you with practical ways to overcome this barrier.

We'll venture together on a journey, straight into the heart of your financial life. We will tackle the importance of starting young, how to set financial goals both short-term and long-term, and the ins-and-outs of budgeting without feeling strangled. We will walk you through managing debts, saving strategically, and introducing you to the world of investing. Later on, we'll focus on risk management, building a solid credit score, attaining financial independence, and much more. Every chapter is a stepping stone to your financial freedom, and it all starts here.

Understanding Money and Wealth

Welcome to the curious world of money and wealth. But remember, understanding money isn't merely about recognizing currency or knowing how to count bills. It encompasses much deeper concepts such as how money is created, how it depreciates and appreciates, along with its overall influence on the economy. On the other hand, wealth, often misconstrued as synonymous with money, is actually the total assets a person owns after deducting all debts and liabilities. Let's peel back these concepts layer by layer.

In basic terms, money is an accepted medium of exchange for goods and services. It is quantified, stored, and traded. However, there's another facet to it — money is a store of value. The money you have in your pocket today should maintain its purchasing power for a significant stretch of time.

Here's where inflation enters the picture. When the cost of goods and services in an economy rises, the purchasing power of the money declines. This is why you can't buy as much with $10 today as you could maybe twenty years ago. When left idle, money depreciates over time, hence the importance of investments to grow and preserve your wealth.

On the flip side, wealth isn't just about having lots of money. It's about having enough resources that would take care of your needs even when you aren't working. Wealth encompasses all the assets you own, minus your debts and liabilities. These assets could be real estate, cash savings, stocks, bonds, mutual funds – just about anything with value.

Wealth accumulation doesn't happen overnight. It requires strategic planning, making informed financial decisions, persistence, and most importantly, time. If you can understand this, you're already on the right path to build your wealth.

Speaking of time, this is where the concept of time value of money (TVM) surfaces. In simple terms, TVM means your dollar today is worth more than the same dollar in future because money can earn interest over time - a concept we'll go into more in the second chapter.

Imagine if you have $10,000 today and you invest it safely to earn an interest rate of 5% yearly. At the end of the year, your money has grown to $10,500. This illustrates the earning potential of money over time, driving home the point why it's smarter to invest money than to keep it idle.

Building on this, investments are an integral part of wealth creation. Whenever you invest, you're essentially putting your money to work. Your money is not only retained but also generates more money by earning interest or appreciating in value.

Now, you may think, "That's easy, I'll just go invest in something!" It's not quite so simple. Investing comes with risks and rewards — a few bad investment choices can result in substantial financial losses. The goal is to find the balance between risk and return that suits your financial goals and risk tolerance.

Apart from making smart investment decisions, building wealth also requires effective management of your income and expenses. This means devising a realistic budget, adhering to it, saving consistently, and creating an emergency fund — all of which we'll cover later in the book.

Understanding the difference between "wants" and "needs" also plays a significant role in wealth accumulation. Living beyond your means by spending more on your "wants" than your "needs" can deter you from stacking wealth. Embracing frugality and spending wisely aids in preserving and growing your wealth.

Briefly, understanding good and bad debts is also crucial. Good debts are ones that can possibly pay off in the future, like a student loan or a mortgage. Bad debts, on the other hand, are often used to purchase disposable items or depreciating assets which don't contribute to your long-term wealth.

Finally, remembering that wealth isn't just a number — it's a culture. It's about making smart financial choices, consistently. It doesn't matter if you can't spare a huge amount each month, what matters is doing it persistently and wisely. Over time, such efforts have a significant impact in increasing your financial health and stability.

In the next chapters, we'll dive deeper into these concepts to give you practical strategies and steps to manage your money effectively, start saving smartly, and invest wisely. Understanding money and wealth is the first epoch in your journey towards financial freedom. So let's ride this journey together!

Psychological Barrier to Saving

One of the most significant hurdles when it comes to saving money isn't the mathematics or the budget—it's in your head. The psychology of saving can make or break even the most concrete plans. Once we comprehend these barriers and how they influence us, we can start to strategize ways of countering them to build strong saving habits.

First, let's tackle one of the most common psychological barriers—instant gratification. In today's fast-paced world, we're used to getting what we want when we want it. This expectation can become a persistent enemy of saving. We prefer to spend money now rather than saving it for unseen future benefits. Although it feels good to buy something new or indulge in a pricey night out, this fleeting pleasure can leave your savings goals in the dust.

Another psychological barrier is the habit to procrastinate. No matter how important your saving goals are, it seems there's always something more urgent that needs your attention first. The problem with this mindset is that the perfect time to start saving never seems to arrive, which leads to last-minute panic or difficulties when an unforeseen expense arises.

Next, we have what's called the 'mental accounting' bias. Basically, it's a tendency to value certain dollars differently than other dollars. For example, you might feel more justified in overspending with your credit card than from your checking account, or you may count an unexpected windfall as 'extra' money rather than incorporating it into your regular saving plan.

The scarcity mindset also plays a huge role in obstructing saving opportunities. This means we often focus on what we don't have, rather than what we do. Not only does this mindset keep us from seeing potential saving opportunities, over time, it can develop into a belief that it's impossible to save or to break out of a cycle of debt.

Now the big question is, how can you overcome these psychological barriers? One key step is to swap instant gratification for delayed gratification. Consider waiting for 24 hours before making large purchases or implementing the '7-day rule,' whereby if you still want a particular item after a week, you'll consider buying it. Delaying impulse buying creates time to reevaluate your decision, which often leads to more saving.

Conquer procrastination by turning saving into an automatic process. Instead of waiting for the perfect moment, set up a routine that automatically transfers a portion of every paycheck into your savings account. This turns saving into a hard-to-break habit, no matter how busy you get.

Another strategy is to reframe scarcity into abundance. Sure, everyone doesn't have an unlimited amount of resources. But instead of focusing on what you don't have, try focusing on what you can do with what you have. Small, regular saving combined with mindful budgeting can lead to surprising growth in your saving potential.

To break the mental accounting bias, treat all money equally, whether it's from your paycheck, a windfall, or your credit card. Incorporate unexpected income into your saving plans instead of viewing it as 'extra' money to spend. In the same vein, remember that credit money isn't 'free' money—it's your future income that you're borrowing.

Last but not least, remind yourself of your bigger saving goals. Whether it's a down payment on your dream house, starting your own business, or a comfy retirement, keeping these goals fresh in mind can make it easier to say no to impulsive spending. You'll feel more motivated to save when you can visualize the long-term payoff of your discipline and patience.

In the end, breaking the psychological barriers to saving takes practice and time. If you slip and overspend or miss a saving goal, don't beat yourself up. Use it as a learning experience and move forward. The sooner you begin to truly understand your mental roadblocks to saving, the sooner you can start smashing through them toward a more secure financial future.

Chapter 1: The Importance of Starting Young

If there's one point to drill into your head, it's this: start young, start now. You're already ahead of many by landing on this book in your 20s. Why? Because good ole' time is your best mate when it comes to stacking cash. It's not just about throwing few bills into a savings account and sitting back, oh no. It's about the magic of compound interest. Amazing stuff, compound interest. It's a bit like a snowball – small at the start, but as it rolls down the slope, gathering more and more snow, things escalate quickly. You invest money, it earns interest, and then that money and interest earn more interest. It's like a financial inception. The earlier you start, the more time your investment snowball has to grow. You may not be rolling in dough right away, but letting that snowball roll while you're young could mean a cushy retirement and a financial safety net. Plus, starting early gives you more time to learn, to ride out the not-so-great times, and to cash in on the good times. It gives your money a chance—for want of a better word— to bloom. So, to recap, the super-secret, exclusive formula for financial freedom: start young and let compound interest do its job. Simple, right?

The Power of Compound Interest

When it comes to building wealth over time, there's one key item that you can't overlook: the power of compound interest. While it may sound like a complicated financial term, it's really quite simple, and understanding it can make all the difference in your financial future.

Let's start with a basic definition. Compound interest is the interest you earn on both your original money and on the interest you continually stack up. This is the magic of compounding: your money grows at an increasing rate.

Let's say you invest $1,000 at an annual interest rate of 5%. After a year, you'll have $1,050. That's your original deposit, plus $50 in interest. If you leave that money in your account, then by the end of the second year, you'll have $1,102.50. That extra $2.50, my friends, is compound interest. You earned interest not just on your initial $1,000, but also on the $50 in interest you accrued previously.

While $2.50 might not sound earth-shattering, imagine that process magnified by larger quantities of money and longer periods of time. That's where it gets really interesting, and you start to see the power of compound interest.

Compound interest is particularly beneficial if you start early. The sooner you can start saving and investing, the more time your money has to compound and grow. This concept ties nicely into the principal of 'time value of money', which essentially means that a dollar today is worth more than a dollar tomorrow, simply because of the potential earning power.

One example of compound interest at work is a retirement savings account. Let's imagine that you open a retirement account at age 20 and contribute $200 every month. Assuming an average return of 7% per year - quite achievable with a well-diversified investment portfolio -, by age 60, you'd have contributed a total of $96,000 to your retirement. However, your account balance wouldn't be $96,000. It would be well over $500,000. That explosive growth is all thanks to the power of compound interest.

It's understandable to question why you should start saving now when there are likely many fun things you can spend on in your 20s. The answer here is all about balance. Yes, enjoy your money now, but also think long term. And the best part? You don't even need a lot of money to harness the power of compound interest. A small, consistent amount saved and invested over time can lead to substantial growth.

Compound interest is also a reason to stay invested during market downturns. The reason here is that if you're earning compound interest, you'll not only recover losses, but continue to grow your capital as the market recovers. This is, of course, assuming you're investing in solid companies or industries that will weather the downturn.

It's vital to remember that compound interest is a double-edged sword. While it can work powerfully in your favor when you're investing, it can act against you when you're in debt. Credit card debt is a stark example where the principle of compound interest can work against you. It's why debts can sometimes feel like they're spiraling out of control, as the interest compounds over time.

On a more positive note, the key takeaway here is that compound interest can turn even the smallest savings into a large sum over time. The secret is consistency and discipline. Make regular contributions, leave the money to grow, and wait. Patience is a secret weapon in building wealth, especially when combined with compound interest.

This power of compound interest is not a secret. It's been famously quoted by Einstein as the eighth wonder of the world. However, it's also one of the most under-utilized concepts in personal finance. Now that you're equipped with this knowledge, don't leave this tool unused. Start saving, start investing, and let compound interest work its magic on your financial future.

Building wealth doesn't always require significant risk or gambling on the latest hot investment. Sometimes, it's as simple as understanding the financial basics, like the power of compound interest, and using them to your advantage. As you move forward on your financial journey, keep the power of compound interest in mind. Nurture it, respect it, and watch it work wonders on your behalf.

Advantages of Starting Early

Just as we turned the page from understanding the power of compound interest, it's vital not to overlook the sheer benefits having time on your side brings to your financial journey. The universe itself can't reverse the clock, but for those who are starting their financial journey young, like you, adding 'time' to your arsenal is a strategic move. So, let's dive into why starting early matters.

For starters, time buys you flexibility. When you get your financial game moving at an early stage, it can present room to correct any financial errors you make. You can experiment, fail and get back on your feet due to the cushioning of time. Your investment strategy doesn't need to be perfect right out of the gate. In fact, it likely won't be. And that's okay.

Consider the analogy of planting a tree. When planted young, the tree has time to weather the storms, withstand varying temperatures and, over time, it grows into a sturdy, reliable entity. The same goes for your finances. Dropping a seed in your early twenties allows it to sprout, weather market fluctuations, and come out robust on the other side.

Another major advantage is that you get to have a longer horizon for risk-taking. Starting early provides you with valuable years to explore high-risk and high-reward investments. As time goes on and responsibilities inch up, your capacity for high risk will naturally decrease. However, the early years allow you to confidently invest in riskier assets, such as stocks or startup businesses, which can potentially yield big returns.

Aside from the investment perspective, starting early on solid financial habits gives you a leg up in understanding wealth management. It's one thing to make money, but it's an entirely different game to maintain and grow that fortune. By starting to save and invest early, you're getting a head start in mastering the art of financial planning and management.

On a more practical level, having a solid financial foundation early on can grant you certain freedoms. There's a peace of mind that accompanies having financial backup. It could be the freedom to change careers, start a business, go for further education, travel, or even take some time off work. Having started early, you won't have to wait until retirement to taste this kind of liberation.

And speaking of retirement, remember it's not strictly an elderly thing. Starting early on your financial journey places a feasible early retirement on the table. This doesn't strictly mean stopping work forever, it could simply mean being able to choose when and where you work. This is financial independence defined; and guess what, starting early makes it a definite possibility.

Furthermore, as you start to build wealth at an early age, it opens doors to opportunities that wouldn't be available otherwise. From investing in real estate to venture capital, early wealth building provides the keys to doors that otherwise might remain closed.

Remember, though, that starting early also ensures that you become financially literate at a young age. This doesn't just mean understanding how to read a balance sheet or compare interest rates. It's about understanding how money works, how to leverage it, how to avoid common mistakes, and how to capitalize on opportunities that come your way.

Moreover, by starting early, you can take advantage of what's often referred to as the 'eighth wonder of the world': compound interest. The power of compound interest magnifies over time. The earlier you start saving and investing, the more compound interest works in your favor. It's like a snowball effect: a tiny snowball rolling from the top of a hill becomes massive at the bottom due to the compounding of snow. The hill is time and you are at the top.

Lastly, but anything but least, beginning your journey to financial freedom early empowers you to weather financial crises more effectively. In life, rainy days are inevitable. Having a sturdy financial umbrella, painstakingly built over the years, can shield you and your loved ones from getting drenched.

All in all, starting early on your journey towards financial independence is not just a good idea; it's the most strategic move you can make. It's not just about getting rich but about giving yourself the freedom and capacity to live the life you want. Your twenties are an exciting time, and setting the foundation for a solid financial future now will only amplify the excitement of the years to come.

Well, now that we've tackled the reasons why it's essential to start young, it's time to discuss the next important step:

setting financial goals. As we move on to the next chapter, let's dive into the multiple ways we can strategize our financial planning, be it short term, long term, or even retirement goals. Remember, starting early can lead to achieving financial milestones earlier than expected.

Chapter 2: Setting Financial Goals

Now that we've already discussed the power of starting early, let's take it a step further by walking you through the process of organizing your financial aspirations into clear and achievable goals. This isn't a one-size-fits-all operation, and you're gonna need short-term, mid-term, and long-term goals that cater to your personal financial situation and life ambitions. Short-term goals are immediate, usually within a year's reach—think saving for a vacation or paying off a credit card. Long-term goals take several years to accomplish; down payment for a house or investing in a start-up can be examples. Retirement goals that are even longer term aim for long-term financial security. Balancing these different goals will keep you stimulated, yet patient, which is key to your financial success. The goal is to make your money work for you so that you're not always working for your money. It's about turning those Benjamins into your own personal army of wealth builders. So, let's map out some stepping stones on this Yellow Brick road to financial freedom, shall we?

Short Term Goals

Let's continue our journey by focusing on the lifeline of your financial planning: your short-term goals. These aren't pie-in-the-sky dreams or distant ambitions. Instead, these are targets and objectives you plan on achieving in the next one to five years. You might wonder why we emphasize short-term goals when financial freedom is often viewed as a long-term, big-picture accomplishment. Well, your larger goals start right here, my friend, with these short-term endeavors.

Short-term goals serve a triple-purpose; they help you stay organized, motivated, and on track. They give you immediate targets to aim for and tangible wins to celebrate. Even better, they create the quick financial wins that build momentum towards the bigger financial picture in your future.

So, what kind of examples could fall under short-term goals? It could be saving up for a vacation, bulk up your emergency fund, paying off a credit card, saving for a new laptop, or even reducing your daily cappuccino expenditure. Whatever it is, it's a goal you can accomplish in a relatively short timeframe and will make a meaningful difference in your financial situation.

Now here's something important to remember. Your short-term goals need to be specific, measurable, achievable, relevant, and time-bound – the famous SMART technique. Instead of saying, "I want to save more money," make it more explicit. Say, "I want to save $500 in three months." This way, you know exactly what you're working toward, and when you plan on getting there.

Next, let's talk about how to prioritize your short-term goals. What determines the importance of each goal? This is subjective and depends largely on your values. However, it's wise to take care of financial liabilities or secure stability before focusing on pleasure-oriented goals. For example, creating a healthy emergency fund might take priority over saving up for that brand new phone.

Your short-term savings should ideally be kept in a safe and easily accessible place. We're certainly not recommending burying it in the backyard or stashing it under your bed. But perhaps putting it in a high-yield savings account, where you can earn a bit of interest while your money sits, could be a good move.

Remember, it's essential to treat your short-term savings as sacred. Resist the urge to dip into them for daily expenses or whimsical wants. Remember, each withdrawal is a step away from that goal. Remember, discipline today equals financial growth tomorrow.

We can't stress enough the importance of automating your short-term savings. Set up a plan where a certain amount goes directly from your paycheck into your short-term savings account. Before you know it, you'll be meeting those targets without even thinking about it. It's like running a marathon with one step at a time, each step getting you closer to the finish line.

Now, all this planning won't do much good if you're not holding yourself accountable. That's where budgeting takes center stage. It's a tool that helps you stay on your set path, reminding you when you might be veering off. Kind of like a lighthouse showing you the safe harbor in the stormy seas of spending.

And while you're at it, remember to celebrate your wins. Reward yourself each time you hit a short-term goal. No, we're not saying go splurge on a shopping spree. Instead, treat yourself to something special that doesn't break your budget and motivate you to keep up the good work. Remember what we said, discipline today equals financial growth tomorrow? Well, it's always nice to add a bit of fun to the mix!

Lastly, be flexible. Your short-term goals might change with time, situation, or preferences—and that's perfectly okay.

Adjust and recalibrate as you deem necessary. Remember, this is your financial journey, and you're the one driving.

In conclusion, short-term goals are stepping stones towards your financial freedom. They have the power to transform you from a spender to a savvy saver. With a dash of discipline, a spoonful of smart strategy, and a sprinkle of self-belief, you can meet these goals head-on. Remember, every giant oak tree starts from a tiny acorn. That's it. Your short-term goals are those vital acorns. Plant them wisely, nurture them, and watch them grow into the mighty oak of your financial freedom.

Just before we wrap up, here's a pro tip: keep the momentum going. Once a short-term goal has been achieved, replace it with a new one. This way, you're continuously marching toward a brighter, more secure financial future. Because at the end of the day, it's your long-term independence and happiness you're ultimately working towards. Remember, Rome wasn't built in a day, but they were laying bricks every hour.

Long Term Goals

Okay, you've nailed your short-term goals, right? They're realistic, achievable, and in progress. But here's a news flash: In the grand scheme of things, they're merely stepping stones to a much larger picture — your long-term goals. But what are long-term goals, why are they important and how can you set them? These are the questions we'll dive into in this section.

Long-term financial goals differ from short-term goals in their time frame, nature and purpose. Technically, anything that requires over a year to achieve can be considered a long-term goal. Buying a house, saving for retirement, or even paying off a sizable student loan — these all fall into the category of long-term goals.

But long-time goals aren't just about the big expenses. They're also about creating a nest egg, ensuring financial freedom, and making yourself recession-proof. Long-term goals increase your financial security in later life, and without them, you're running the risk of financial distress, particularly given the unpredictability of life.

Importance of Long-Term Goals

Why should you be concerned with long-term plans in your 20s? Simply because this is the crucial decade where the right habits and decisions can set you on the path toward a secure future. The trick is not just working FOR money, but making money work FOR you.

Long-term goals provide direction, motivation but they also aid in making daily life decisions easier. Having a goal means that every financial decision you make today is influenced by the future you'd like to have. Ostensibly, it imposes a good level of self-discipline.

Necessity has the power to funnel down your keyword search from 'latest iPhone release' to 'best investment options for millennials', and that's where you want to be. After all, your future self will thank you.

Setting Long-Term Goals

Now that you understand the gravity of long-term goals, the question remains: how to go about setting them? Again, it's essential here to be SMART (Specific, Measurable, Attainable, Relevant and Time-Bound).

In simpler language, don't just say, "I want to be rich." Instead, say, "I want to save $1 million by the time I'm 50." This is specific, measurable, as well as time-bound. Whether it's attainable or not will depend on your income, your saving and investing strategy.

Investing Towards Long-Term Goals

Let's make something very clear — savings alone are not enough to reach your long-term financial goals. The real key to accumulating wealth lies in investing.

Investing can be scary, especially when you're starting out. Heck, it might sound like gambling to some. It calls for risk tolerance and a stomach for short-term volatility. But it's critical to know that with good advice, sound strategies and a long-term perspective, the benefits of investing far outweigh the short-term risks.

In your 20s, having time on your side means you can afford to be aggressive with your investment choices. Stocks, primarily, can offer impressive returns over the long-term. And thanks to the magic of 'compounding,' even small amounts can snowball into substantial nest eggs over time.

Long-Term Goals and Retirement

Retirement is likely going to be the biggest expense of your life, and it's something that can't be ignored, even in your 20s. Starting to save early can have tremendous benefits.

Think about this: When you're old and your working days are behind you, you'd ideally want to be financially stable, not juggling a part-time job or relying on social security checks. This isn't a state of prosperity; it's a bare-minimum requirement. So start planning for it while it's still early.

Long-Term Goals and Real Estate

Long-term goals can include investing in real estate. However, this requires a significant capital outlay, so it's important to understand when you're in a financial position to make this kind of commitment.

Real estate can provide some fantastic opportunities for building wealth due to appreciation, rental income, and tax advantages. However, it can also present risks if the market drops, or if you end up selling at a loss. So always consider real estate investments very carefully.

Final Thoughts

All of this might seem intimidating, but remember, Rome wasn't built in a day and neither will your financial future be. It's a step-by-step process of creating and implementing plans to achieve your financial goals. There will be setbacks, surprises, and detours, but that's where perseverance comes in.

To round off, the message is this: In your 20s, start focusing on the long game. The ball is in your court, with time as your biggest ally. Use it wisely, invest smartly, and you'll be on your way to a secure and comfortable future. So go ahead, shake those daydreams of financial independence into a glorious reality.

Retirement Goals

After looking at both short term and long term financial goals, now let's tackle the big kahuna: retirement goals. You're probably thinking, "But I'm only in my 20s, why should I even think about retirement now?" The answer is simple: because time equals money.

Don't underestimate the power of starting early. By setting your retirement goals now, you're not only giving yourself a road map for the future, but you're also making the most out of the compound interest. The more time your money has to grow, the better off you'll be. So let's get down to the nitty-gritty of setting those retirement goals.

First, imagine your future self. Where do you want to be when you're 60 or 70? What sort of lifestyle would you like to maintain? Take some time to visualize your retirement years. This will help you set a realistic financial goal.

The next step is to figure out how much you'll need to save each month to reach your goal. The actual amount will depend on a number of factors including your anticipated living expenses, healthcare costs (which tend to increase with age), and any income you may receive from social security or other sources.

To give you an idea, a common rule of thumb is that you'll need about 70-80% of your pre-retirement income to maintain a similar lifestyle in retirement. However, it's worth noting that everyone's circumstances are different, so this is just a ballpark figure.

So, let's say you're currently earning $50,000 a year, and you plan to retire in about 40 years. According to that rule of thumb, you'll need to aim for an annual retirement income of roughly $35,000 to $40,000. It's important to note these numbers should factor in inflation too.

Retirement Saving Methods

Now that you have a target in mind, let's talk about how to save for retirement. There are many different routes you can take, each with its own set of advantages and drawbacks.

One of the most common methods is through employer-sponsored retirement accounts like 401(k)s.

With a 401(k), you can choose to have a portion of your income automatically contributed before taxes. Many employers also offer a matching contribution up to a certain percentage. This essentially represents free money that you should take advantage of, if possible.

If your employer doesn't offer a retirement plan, or if you want to save additional funds for retirement beyond what's possible with your employer's plan, consider opening an Individual Retirement Account (IRA). There are two main types of IRAs: Traditional and Roth. The key difference between them comes down to when you pay taxes.

With a Traditional IRA, you contribute pre-tax dollars and then pay taxes on withdrawals in retirement. With a Roth IRA, you contribute post-tax dollars, so your withdrawals in retirement are tax-free. Both types have their own contribution limits and qualifications, so you'll want to do some research to figure out which option works best for you.

Investing is another method to grow your retirement savings. Remember, it's not enough to just stash your money in a savings account. You need to put your money to work for you. Stocks, bonds, and mutual funds are some of the most popular ways to invest for retirement. However, keep in mind investing involves risks.

Lastly, don't forget about other income sources in retirement like social security, pensions, or rental property income. Social security alone is unlikely to be enough to meet your needs in retirement, but it can certainly be part of your retirement income strategy.

In conclusion, setting retirement goals now, in your 20s, will give you a financial roadmap to follow. Having a clear vision of what you want will motivate you to stay on the right financial path. And remember, starting early gives you the best shot at achieving your retirement dreams. So start investing in your future self today!

Chapter 3: Budgeting Basics

After setting those financial goals, you gotta learn how to make 'em a reality, and no, it can't be all dreams and no action. We're talking budgeting, guys - the cornerstone of all successful financial plans. But don't worry, it won't be as monotonous as it sounds. Think of it this way, budgeting is like having a financial GPS, it guides you on how to distribute your income and helps you track where your cash is going. So, how do you start crafting your budget? Easy. Figure out your monthly income, list all your expenses - both fixed and variable, then do the math. The goal is to ensure your income covers all your expenses and leaves you with some savings. Now, sticking to this budget? That's the real challenge. It's not rocket science though; it's more about discipline and a bunch of willpower. Remember, it's okay to make adjustments along the way - your budget is not set in stone. It's there to assist you, not to constrain you! Now grab a pen and paper or whatever tool works for you and get cracking on that budget plan. It's time to take charge of your finances, don't you think?

Creating a Budget

Just like planting a seed to reap fruits later, that's the first step in your financial freedom journey – creating a budget. It frames your financial picture, providing you with a full view of where your money comes from, how much is there, and where it all ends up.

Begin with tracking your income. Identify all your sources of income, including your paycheck, any interest earned on savings, and additional earnings. Don't just think of your gross income – what really matters is your net income, which means the money that's in your pocket after taxes and other deductions.

Next up, record your expenses. Categorize them into fixed and variable expenses. Fixed expenses include your rent, car payments, or any other costs that don't change month over month. Variable expenses, on the other hand, are susceptible to change and include dining out, shopping, entertainment, and more.

To stay on top of this, make use of technology. There are numerous budgeting apps out there that can make this task much easier. They can digitally categorize your expenses and visually depict where your money is going, even alerting you when you're approaching the limit of your budgetary categories.

Although keeping tabs on every single penny could seem exhaustive, it's definitely worthwhile. It helps you see spending patterns and identify areas where you can cut back. Most people are surprised to discover how much they spend on incidentals like coffee or eating out.

Once you know where your money is going, it's time to set your financial goals– i.e., what do you want your money to do for you? Whether you want to pay off debts or save up for a house down payment, having a clearly defined goal will help structure your budget accordingly.

Now, subtract your total expenditures from your total take-home income. The objective is to have a positive number after doing this calculation. If the number is negative, it means you're spending more than you're earning- a sign telling you to reconsider your spending patterns.

If you ended up with a surplus, that's great! This extra money should be allocated towards your financial goals like paying off a loan or bolstering your retirement savings.

But what if the numbers aren't adding up right? For instance, you need to cut back. An easy way to do this is to employ the 50/30/20 rule by U.S. Senator Elizabeth Warren. In her book, she recommends allocating 50% of your income to needs (rent, groceries), 30% towards wants (eating out, hobbies), and the remaining 20% goes towards savings or debt payments, whichever applicable.

Creating a budget is only successful when you stick to it. The key is to make a budget that's realistic – an over-optimistic budget will likely leave you frustrated, leading to rash financial decisions.

Regularly monitor your budget – at least monthly, and make updates as necessary. Things change – whether it's an increase in rent or a pay raise. Adjustments will need to be made to ensure your budget remains effective.

No matter how meticulously you plan though, unexpected expenses will arise. That's why it's crucial to build an emergency fund, a topic we'll dive deeper into during our discussion on saving strategies.

Creating a budget might seem like a daunting task at first, but remember, it's a tool to empower you. It puts you in control of your financial future. Once you better understand and manage your money, you'll find yourself inching closer to your financial goals.

Remember, it's not about restricting your spending, but rather, making thoughtful decisions and knowing where your hard-earned cash is going. So, aim to create a budget that respects your aspirations - a budget that works for you, not against you.

A well-structured, practical budget indeed paves the way towards managing debts, tactful saving, and smart investing– aspects we'll explore more in the sections to come. So it's time to take the wheel of your financial journey and steer it in the direction of your dreams.

Sticking to your Budget

Now that we've gone over creating a budget, the next crucial step in this journey is sticking to it. Easier said than done, right? However, doing so is possible and could be your game-changer toward achieving financial freedom. Over the next few paragraphs, we'll walk this journey together. So, let's get started.

The first thing to remember is that your budget isn't a prison. It's not supposed to push you to the brink of frustration. Instead, think of it as a guiding light, leading you towards your financial goals. This mindset can help make it a lot less challenging to stick to.

It's also important to regularly check how you're doing with your budget. Make it a habit to review your expenses, say, once a week. This way, you can spot if you're overspending in certain areas and promptly address it. Regular reviews also allow you to make necessary adjustments. Remember, your budget isn't set in stone.

When sticking to your budget, understanding the difference between needs and wants is key. Needs are things that are necessary for survival like food, rent, and healthcare. Wants, on the other hand, are things that are nice to have but not essential. When you're able to distinguish between the two, controlling your spending becomes easier.

Another great technique for sticking to your budget is finding cheaper alternatives. Why buy a new book when you could borrow it from a library for free? Or why not cook at home instead of going out to eat? Small changes like these can have a big impact on your savings.

Delegate a good potions of your budget to savings. This doesn't just mean the money left over after expenses. Make it a rule to save first, then spend what's left. You'll be surprised how this mentality makes sticking to a budget easier.

Utilize technology for tracking your budget. There are numerous budgeting apps out there that can help you keep an eye on your money. These tools can alert you when you're nearing your budget limit and provide helpful insights into your spending habits.

Another important concept is having a buffer in your budget. Life happens — even if you've planned down to the last cent, unexpected expenses can arise. Set aside a part of your budget as a contingency to deal with these surprises.

Learning to say no is an underrated secret to sticking to a budget. Yeah, it can be tough turning down an invitation to binge on a meal out or purchase a fancy gadget. But, being assertive about saying no today can help secure your financial freedom for tomorrow.

Also, be sure to reward yourself at times. Sticking to a budget doesn't mean you can't have fun. Treat yourself to something nice, every once in while, without disrupting your budget. This can reinforce good behavior and make the process more joyous.

Beware of budget busters. These are things that can blindside your budget, like spontaneous purchases and hidden subscription fees. Staying aware of these potential traps can help you avoid them and stick to your budget.

Don't be too hard on yourself if you make mistakes. Nobody's perfect. Even the most disciplined of us can slip up from time to time. The key is to acknowledge the error, learn from it, and get back on the budgeting track.

Create clear, achievable financial goals. This gives you a target to aim for, making it easier to stay focused on sticking to your budget. Want to go on a vacation, buy a new car or maybe even own your home? Having such goals can be just the motivation you need.

Being open about your budget can create accountability. Discuss your budget with a partner, friend, or family member. Just sharing your budget goals can make you more determined to stick to it, because now there's someone else holding you to it.

Lastly, remember that sticking to a budget is like forming a new habit. It might feel hard at first, but with time, it will become a natural part of your lifestyle. Keep reminding yourself of the benefits it brings and don't give up. The journey to financial freedom awaits!

Chapter 4: Managing Debts

After smart budgeting in the last chapter, you are now equipped with spending wisely. But, let's dig into something that's usually swept under the rug - debt. Don't see debt as your enemy but rather as a financial tool that you can command to your advantage. It's crucial to discern between good debts and bad debts. Good debts, like student loans, can be investments. They have potential to produce wealth in the long run. Bad debts, though, which include credit card debts and personal loans, can burden you as their interests compound over time. Here's a piece of advice: always make it a point to balance your debts. Prioritize spending less on liabilities and channeling more toward assets, and always pay your debts on time to avoid accumulating interest. You can also explore debt consolidation or refinancing options, which can bring down interest rates, thus lowering your monthly payments. Time to take control and lead your way out of debts!

Understanding Good and Bad Debt

Up until now, we've covered the basics of budgeting and the importance of starting young with your financial plans. We've helped you understand that not all money management strategies are about saving. Some are about managing what you owe - your debts. Let's dig in and figure out the difference between good and bad debt.

The concept might sound odd, but let's break it down. Not all debt is created equal. Some debts can be advantageous, while others can lead you down a slippery slope towards financial disaster. So, it's crucial that we can discern between the two types.

Good debt is an investment that will grow in value or generate long-term income. The primary goal here is that the loan will eventually pay off, having helped you generate a more significant net value or additional income. Often, good debts come with low-interest rates, making them easier to manage over time and reducing their overall financial impact.

Examples of good debt might include something like a student loan or a home mortgage. With a student loan, you're investing in your education, with the expectation that this education will lead to higher paying jobs in the future. The return on investment here comes in the form of your increased earning potential. Similarly, a mortgage lets you buy more real estate than you can afford upfront, in the hope that the property appreciates over time, leading to wealth creation.

On the flip side of the equation, we have bad debts. These debts tend to have high-interest rates and are used to purchase depreciating assets. The tricky part about such debt is that it decreases your ability to invest in the future."

An example of bad debt is credit card debt used for purchasing consumables or depreciating assets like a new car model. Unlike a home which could appreciate in value over time, a new car starts to depreciate in value as soon as you drive it off the lot.

If you find yourself stuck in a rut with bad debts, rule number one is to not panic. Start by reaching out to your creditors and see if they're willing to negotiate. You then have to establish a payment plan and stick to it. Prioritize the highest interest rate debts first, as they cost you the most.

Another strategy to managing bad debt is to consolidate your debts. This means taking out a new loan with a lower interest rate to pay off high-interest ones. But be warned, this is only a beneficial strategy if it helps you pay off your debt faster. And remember, this works best if you don't add more debt on top of it.

Prevention, however, is by far the best method to manage bad debt. It's essential to understand the difference between wants and needs. Remember, having the latest gadgets or wardrobe often results in needless spending and, consequently, more debt. Living within your means and having an iron-clad budget that you pledge to stick to is one of the best protection strategies against bad debt.

Loans and credit are useful tools when used wisely. They provide opportunities to invest in significant life improvements and wealth-creating assets. Being smart about which kinds of debts you decide to take on can make all the difference when it comes to your financial stability and independence. Keep in mind that good debt helps you grow your wealth, while bad debt can shrink it.

Finally, let's not forget about our overall financial goals. You should always be aware of how your debts, good or bad, fit into your broader financial strategy. Before taking on debt, consider whether it fits into your short-term and long-term financial goals and how it impacts your ability to save and invest for the future.

We hope this section served as an eye-opener for you about good and bad debt. Remember, debts, like money itself, are just tools in your broader financial toolkit. Used wisely, they can be a stepping-stone to financial freedom. But using them without understanding their structure, rates, and long-term costs can set you back significantly on your path to financial independence.

Next, we'll delve into steps you can take to balance debts and set up a well-rounded financial plan. You've mastered the understanding of good and bad debt, now it's time to take action.

Steps to Balancing Debts

Now that we've covered the basics of understanding good and bad debts, it's time to take a closer look at how to balance these debts. As efficient and practical as budgeting might be, it won't take you far if your debts are out of control. Here are the steps you need to follow to keep your debts under control.

The first step towards balancing your debts is understanding exactly what you owe. This may sound trivial, but in reality, it's surprising how many people have a hazy idea of their actual debt figures. Compile a list of all your debts: student loans, credit card balances, car loans, mortgages, or any other obligations. Calculate how much you owe, what interests you're paying, and to whom it's owed. You can't make a plan without knowing your starting point.

Following that, you have to set clear repayment priorities. When it comes to balancing debt, not all debts are created equal. Paying off a high-interest credit card balance should take priority over a low-interest student loan. By prioritizing your debts based on interest rates, you'll save money in the long run by reducing the amount of interest you pay over time.

Thirdly, come up with a viable payment plan. This involves allocating a certain portion of your income towards debt reduction. Two popular methods are the "snowball" method, where you start by paying off the smallest debt first, and the "avalanche" method, where you start with the debt with the highest interest rate. Both methods come with their unique advantages and the choice between them will depend on your personal circumstances and your psychological makeup.

Another essential step in debt balancing is to stop accumulating new debt. The temptation can be strong, but if you want to dig yourself out of the hole, you have to stop digging first. That's not to say that you shouldn't use credit at all, instead use it wisely. Think twice before you swipe your card and avoid falling into the spending trap due to the allure of reward points.

The next step is crafting a budget, which we discussed in the previous chapter. A budget is impossible to overlook when you're seeking to balance your debts. It outlines your income, expenses, and gives you a tangible plan on how to allocate your funds. By sticking to your budget, you can be certain your money is being directed where it needs to be - towards reducing your debt.

Contingency plans are a must. Life happens. Emergencies crop up. Being prepared for the unexpected is critical to maintaining a balanced debt load. It's essential to have an emergency fund as a buffer against sudden life crises that could derail your repayment schedules. Without a contingency plan, these moments can plunge you further into debt.

Another significant step is to maintain good relationships with your creditors. If you find yourself in a tough financial spot, it's easier to negotiate terms with a creditor with which you have a good working relationship. They might be willing to adjust your payment plan, lower your interest rate or waive late fees, providing much-needed relief on your debt journey.

Avoiding minimum payments is a step most people miss. When you pay the minimum due on credit cards, you're mostly just paying off the interest and barely making a dent in the principal. If you can, always strive to pay more than the bare minimum. This step will take you that much closer to eliminating your debts fast.

If your debts are overwhelming, consider seeking professional help. There are numerous credit counseling organizations that can provide guidance. They can help negotiate with creditors, lower your interest rates, waive fees, and consolidate your debts into a single, manageable monthly payment.

Another vital step is to constantly evaluate and adjust your plans. Financial circumstances are like a river, they are always changing. It's essential to review your payment plans and budgets periodically, adjusting them as your financial condition changes. You might get a new job with a higher salary, receive a windfall, or experience an unexpected expenditure. Your plans should adjust accordingly.

A consolidation loan might provide that much-needed lifeline if you're drowning in multiple debts. This step involves taking out one loan to pay off all your other debts, which simplifies repayment. Essentially, you'll be left with one loan payment to manage, typically at a lower interest rate. However, proceed with caution and be certain you understand all the terms and costs involved before using this strategy.

Keep track of your progress. Charting your progress as you pay down your debts can be a great motivator. It can also help you identify trends and areas where you can increase payment or reduce spending. You can follow your progress by manually tracking your payments, or utilizing apps designed specifically for this function.

The next step? Celebrate your wins, no matter how small. While it's important to stay focused on your long-term financial goals, allowing yourself to enjoy your progress reinforces your intent to become debt-free. Remember, this is as much about altering bad spending habits as it is about paying what you owe. Positive reinforcement is an excellent way to make new habits stick.

The final step in all this is patience. Balancing debts isn't something achieved overnight. You took time to accumulate these debts, it will take time to clear them out. But with patience, determination, and adherence to the steps mentioned above, you will find yourself steadily moving towards a financially balanced life with a manageable debt load.

Chapter 5: Saving Strategies

After learning about managing debts in the previous chapter, let's now focus on strategies to turbocharge your savings. Create an emergency fund first and foremost. This fund will be your financial cushion, able to cover at least three to six months of living expenses, so you can weather unexpected expenses without sinking into debt. Once you've got that sorted, look at saving accounts. Not all are created equal – find one with the best interest rates and lowest fees to max out your savings. Lastly, consider utilizing automatic saving. By setting up automatic transfers straight from your paycheck to your savings account, you're taking the thought out of saving. It becomes an unconscious habit, and before you know it, your savings will have grown significantly. Remember, the goal isn't just to save money, but to grow it over time – so don't let your money just sit there, make it work for you!

Emergency Funds

So, you've learned the basics of budgeting and have begun to dip your toes into the world of savings. Now let's get into something you need to prioritize - creating an emergency fund. You might think, "Why should I tied up my money for rainy days?" But hey, life's unpredictable! An emergency fund acts as a safety net when life throws a financial curveball your way.

Let's start off by defining an emergency fund. In its simplest terms, an emergency fund is a stash of money set aside to cover the financial surprises life throws your way. These unexpected events can be stressful and costly. Here are some examples: you lose your job, your car breaks down, or you get sick or injured.

So, why is having an emergency fund important? Firstly, it covers unexpected costs. This means that if something does go wrong, you can't end up in a cycle of debt trying to pay back the money you had to borrow. Furthermore, it provides peace of mind. Believe me, there's nothing worse than fretting about how you'll manage financially when dealing with an emergency. But, with an emergency fund in place, you can quickly divert your full attention to the job, health or personal issue at hand.

Now, the pressing question - how much money should you have in your emergency fund? A good rule is to aim for three to six months of living expenses. Calculate the amount based on your personal circumstances including your monthly bills and daily expenses. The ideal emergency fund size can vary, but it should be enough to give you the peace of mind you need to know that emergencies won't leave you in debt.

How do you build this emergency fund, especially when you're just starting out in your career? It's not always easy, but it's not impossible. Begin by setting monthly saving goals. Even if you start small, it's progress. Whether that's $50, $100, or more, consistency is key. As your income increases, you can gradually increase this monthly amount as well.

Remember, the key to achieving any financial goal - including building your emergency fund - is to be realistic and patient. Acknowledge that it might take you a while to reach your emergency fund goal. That's okay. Don't get disheartened, your perseverance will pay off.

You might be wondering where to keep your emergency fund. It should be easily accessible, but not too accessible where you might be tempted to dig into it for non-emergencies. Consider opening a separate savings account specifically for this purpose. Look for a high-yield savings account for the best bang for your buck, allowing your emergency fund to grow slowly over time.

One important rule is to use your emergency fund only for emergencies. This doesn't mean dipping into it for an impromptu vacation plan or for that shiny new gadget you've been eying. It's there to be used for significant unexpected expenses, job loss, or medical bills. Learning to differentiate between needs and wants plays a crucial role here.

Once you've built up your emergency fund, don't get complacent. Reevaluate and replenish it as needed, especially if you've had to draw from it. It's not a "set it and forget it" situation; you should continually maintain and adjust it as necessary depending on your financial situation and living expenses.

Building an emergency fund may seem like a daunting task, but it's a crucial element to your overall financial health. It's not just about making saving a habit; it's about understanding the importance of safeguarding your future from the unpredictability of life.

So far, we've learned how to budget our money, manage our debts, set saving strategies, and make an emergency fund. Now, we can move on to the next exciting part - investing. Investing is another effective way to save for the future because it allows your money to grow substantially over a period. In the next chapter, we will discuss different types of investments, their risks, and their potential rewards.

But for now, give yourself a pat on the back for reaching this point. You're not just dreaming about financial security; you're actively working towards it. Your 20's is the perfect time to lay the groundwork for a future of financial wellness, and creating an emergency fund is a solid step in that direction. Cheers towards making smart financial decisions!

Saving Accounts

The moment you've learned about budgeting and setting up your emergency fund, it's time to consider another key element of your financial security - saving accounts. This tool is a nearly timeless staple in the world of money management, a classic that has seen people through thick and thin. So, what's all the big deal about it, and why should you prioritize having one? Let's dive in.

Quite simply put, saving accounts are a safe way to keep your hard-earned cash while also earning some interest. But it's not just about storing money. It also involves making your money work for you. It's a secure place for your money to grow, albeit, at a modest rate. However, in the world of finance, something is always better than nothing.

Hence, keeping your money in a savings account isn't just about security; it's about building your wealth systematically and steadily. Think of it as an extremely patient turtle in the race of finance. It may be slow, but it's a definite and steady way to the finish line. Ensuring you get there is our main goal, of course.

When selecting a savings account, there are a few essential factors to consider. First, look at the interest rates. These are usually presented as an Annual Percentage Yield (APY) — a higher APY means your money works harder and earns more for you. Savings accounts can vary widely in this aspect, so make sure to compare different options.

Second, consider the minimum balance requirement. Some savings accounts require a certain amount to be maintained in the account. If it's too high, it might not be feasible for you, especially if you're just starting on your savings journey.

Also, consider the ease of access you have to your money. While the point of a savings account is to keep money safe and let it grow, life can throw curveballs, and you may need to access those funds. So, it's critical to understand how easily you can withdraw your money when needed.

Keep in mind - there can be limits on the number of withdrawals you can make within a certain timeframe. Exceeding this limit may incur penalties or fees which can eat into your earned interest. You wouldn't want that, right? So, make sure to know the limitations before you dive into any savings account.

Notably, technology has brought in a wave of online savings accounts as well. They're often run by virtual banks without physical branches. One upside to this is that they tend to offer higher interest rates because they save on the overhead costs associated with running physical branches. So, it's worth looking into these if the idea of a digital bank suits you.

Moreover, several savings accounts are designed specifically with certain goals in mind. You've got accounts like the education savings accounts, retirement savings accounts, and health savings accounts. Each come with their unique benefits and can be invaluable tools in reaching specific long-term financial goals.

Ultimately, having a savings account adds another layer of security to your financial assets. There's an extra cushion between you and any potential financial emergencies that could come up. Plus, they can link to your checking account for regular, automated transfers to make saving feel seamless.

Now, let's debunk a myth: Setting up a savings account is complex. No, it's not! It's as easy as choosing any other service or product; you need to look around, compare options, understand your needs, and make an informed decision.

So, there you have it. Saving accounts are a necessary tool in your finance toolkit. Sure, they're not as flashy as stocks or real estate. But they provide a safe, reliable way for your money to grow. They're the dependable friend who's always there, only in this case, that friend is there to help you grow your wealth.

As in everything else in finance, don't put all your eggs in one basket. A savings account is just one facet of your varying savings strategies. Use it wisely and in conjunction with other methods like investing. Your 20s are the perfect time to start building this financial fortress to secure your future.

Remember, the key is to start now. Every penny saved is a penny earned and a penny that can grow. Let's keep the momentum going, alright?

Utilizing Automatic Saving

Now that we've got a handle on emergency funds and savings accounts, let's jump straight into the magic of automatic saving. Essentially, automatic saving refers to a financial strategy in which a specified amount of money is automatically transferred from your checking account to your savings account on a regular basis. This might sound quite straightforward, yet its potency in achieving financial independence can't be underestimated.

Though the concept of automatic saving is simple, it can have profound effects on your financial health. It's similar to "setting and forgetting"; the difference is, you're setting your finances on a path that builds wealth without constant intervention on your part.

Picture this: every month, even before you can touch your paycheck—a portion of it is already squirreled away into your savings. Yep, right off the bat, you're taking care of your future. And the best part is, you're less likely to miss money that you never saw in your account in the first place!

Automatic saving aids in preventing the temptation that comes with spending money just because it's there. It's an effective way to enforce disciplined saving without the stress of manually transferring money each month.

The beauty also lies in the flexibility of automatic saving. You're not required to deposit a large chunk of money. Start with small amounts, and as your budget allows, gradually increase it over time. The key here is consistency; even small, regular deposits to a savings account can grow substantially over time due to compound interest that we discussed in Chapter 1.

Setting Up Automatic Saving

It's as easy as pie to set up automatic saving with most banks or credit unions. It typically involves a simple online process where you set a designated amount and frequency (weekly, biweekly, or monthly) for the automatic transfers.

If for some reason your bank doesn't offer automatic saving, don't get discouraged. Third-party applications also offer services that automatically transfer money to a saving account. Apps like Digit and Acorns can detect your spending habits and automatically save suitable amounts accordingly.

It's critical to set your automatic savings to coincide with your payday. This ensures you won't accidentally overdraw on your account and have a sufficient balance prior to the transfer. It also ensures that your future saving is prioritized over any other spending.

To Infinity and Beyond

Take the time to regularly review your budget, as we covered in Chapter 3. As your income grows, so too should your automatic savings amount. It's fascinating to observe how your savings can grow incrementally over time, merely by maintaining this one habit. And who said making progress wasn't thrilling?

The goal of automatic saving is to make saving money an effortless task for you. However, the easy set-and-forget nature doesn't mean you should completely overlook your savings. It's still important to keep tabs on your savings progress and revisit your savings goals regularly. Maintaining an active role in your finances is key to staying motivated and reaching your goals.

Paving the Path Towards Investing

Automatic saving can serve as a foundation for more intricate financial strategies like investing. Once you have a steady amount going into your savings each month, consider diverting a part of it towards investments. It's about balancing the safety of saving while dipping your toes in the more risky world of investments. Just remember, risks should be taken in calculated measures.

You can utilize automatic savings not just for emergency funds, but also for specific investment goals. Whether you're saving for stocks, bonds, or mutual funds, automatic saving can help you accumulate the capital needed to take your first investment step. We'll learn more about these investment options in Chapter 6.

No financial strategy is one-size-fits-all. The right approach depends on your financial situation, your goals, and your comfort level with saving and investing. Automatic saving, however, provides a universal method for consistently growing your wealth, enabling financial freedom and the flexibility to explore other financial opportunities.

Lastly, don't forget that financial freedom isn't an instantaneous result. It's a continuous journey that requires you to form and uphold habits like automatic saving over time. Even if it seems slow paced at first, don't be discouraged. Remember, the tortoise did end up winning the race.

Chapter 6: Introduction to Investing

Okay, so you've got a killer budget, you're chipping away at your debt, and your savings are starting to grow—that's great! But if you want to seriously increase your wealth, you need to step into the world of investing. Now, don't panic. It's not as complex or intimidating as some might think. It's all about purchasing assets today with the hope that they will increase in value over time, helping your money to grow at a rate that outspeeds inflation. There are various avenues for you to make investments including stocks, bonds, mutual funds, and real estate. Each carries its own benefits, risks, and degrees of hand-on involvement. This chapter is all set to be a beginner's guide to introduce you to these concepts and help you dip your toes into the waters of investing. You don't have to be a Wall Street guru to get started. Remember, knowledge and time are your best allies when it comes to successful investing, so let's get into it!

Stocks

Coming from a solid grasp of understanding the basics of investing, we're now ready to delve deeper. It's time to talk about stocks, an exciting venture that's often synonymous with the classic image of wealth accumulation.

First of all, when you buy a stock, you're buying a piece of a company. It's like owning a slice of pizza from a large pie. That 'slice' gives you the right to share in the company's success through dividends and capital appreciation. You become a part-owner of that company. Groovy, isn't it?

The value of your stock fluctuates, going up or down, depending on several factors. These factors include the company's financial health, market demand for their products or services, and overall economic conditions. It could also be affected by investors' perceptions of the industry or broader stock market trends.

Investing in stocks can be a viable pathway to financial freedom, especially if you get started in your 20s. The best part is that stocks have historically outperformed other investments in the long run. Yeah, we're talking decades here.

Now, you might be wondering, "How do I start investing in stocks?" Here's where brokerage accounts come into play. A brokerage account, simply put, is like a bank account but for your investments. An online brokerage is an easy-to-navigate platform that allows you to buy and sell stocks.

It's also essential to learn about the two primary methods of profiting from stocks—capital gains and dividends. Capital gains occur when you sell a stock for more than you paid for it. Dividends are bits of the company's earnings paid out to shareholders. They can be a steady stream of income and can even be reinvested to acquire more shares.

But hey, investing in stocks is not a venture without risks. The stock market is volatile, meaning it can swing up or down drastically in a short span. Some people even lose a chunk of their investments when the market goes south. So it's important not to put all your eggs in the stocks basket.

This is where the concept of diversification is brought into conversation. It's basically spreading your investments among different types of assets to manage risks. Picture it like not betting your entire fortune on one hand of poker; you spread the bets to improve your chances of winning.

Also, pay attention to fees. Certain amounts are required to buy and sell stocks. There are transaction costs, commission fees, and potential account maintenance charges that can eat into your returns if not clearly understood and managed.

Despite the risks, many people are drawn to investing in stocks due to their potential for high return rates. And let's not forget about compound interest. When you start investing young, your earnings begin to generate their own earnings. It's like watching your money have baby dollars— now, isn't that a sight to see?

A little insider tip for you, investing in companies you're familiar with can be a savvy strategy. Knowing their business processes and services can provide you with valuable insights into the stock's growth potential.

Another crucial point is to stay committed to your financial goals. Regardless if your goal is for short-term gains or for long-term investments like retirement planning, having a clear vision helps you stay focused and less swayed by the market's fluctuating nature.

Lastly, keep your emotions in check. The stock market frequently ups and downs are bound to stir up emotions. But here's the thing, impulsive decisions based on fear or greed rarely pay off. Stay cool, calm, and collected. Insightful strategy wins over turbulence.

Being engaged in stocks brings us closer to financial freedom. With proper understanding, awareness, and a disciplined approach, this exciting world of stocks can open up vast opportunities for wealth accumulation.

Bonds

And presto, just like that, we've hit the sweet spot of classic investing that's been around since time immemorial - Bonds. Bonds are like the much older, responsible sibling of stocks. They're less risky, more predictable and might just be exactly what you need to kick-start that road to financial freedom.

So, what precisely are bonds? At its core, buying a bond is like lending money to the government or a company. You're basically playing the bank, and that makes you kind of a big deal. Like a loan, bonds have an end (or "maturity") date when the sum should be paid back in full. Until then, interest payments are made to you, the bondholder. Now, you're not only getting the green back but it's growing too.

One of the key things with bonds is the inverse relationship they have with interest rates. Let's break it down. When interest rates go up, bond prices go down. Why is that? Well, if new bonds are issued with higher interest rates, then the older, lower-interest bonds look a lot less appealing, don't they? Hence, their prices drop. Watch out for this give and take when you're contemplating investing in bonds.

Let's get into the types of bonds out there. There are government bonds, municipal bonds, corporate bonds, just to name a few. Government bonds are generally considered the safest, with the U.S treasury bonds leading the pack in terms of security. Municipal bonds are issued by local municipalities, while corporate bonds are issued by companies. Choose your bonds wisely based on the level of risk you're comfortable with.

Treasury bonds are typically viewed as the safest investment. That's right! Safer than your money under the mattress. These bonds are backed by the full faith and the credit of the

U.S. government, so unless Uncle Sam goes bankrupt, you're getting your cash back. Interest from these babies is also federally tax-free, giving you more bang for your buck.

Corporate bonds, on the other hand, tend to carry more risk and offer higher interest rates compared to government bonds. Remember, higher potential return usually comes with higher risk—no such thing as a free lunch in the financial world.

Municipal bonds are a sweet middle ground. They offer moderate default risk but carry the advantage of interest that's usually free from federal income taxes and sometimes state and local taxes too, depending on where you live.

Now, where do you buy bonds? You can purchase bonds directly from the issuer (for instance, the U.S. government or a company), or from other investors just like you. Additionally, you can buy bond mutual funds or exchange-traded funds (ETFs) which simply pool investments in a variety of bonds. It's like an all-you-can-eat bond buffet.

Before you jump into the bond world, it's paramount that you understand bond ratings—these are scores given to bonds that tell potential investors how risky a bond is. When a company or government issues a bond, a bond rating company like Moody's or Standard & Poor's gives it a score based on the entity's financial stability. The higher the score, the less risk associated with investing in the bond.

But here's the key thing with bonds you need to know: unlike Stocks, with bonds, you know what's coming to you. It's literally written into the deal – The frequency of interest payments, the interest rate, and the face value you'll get back when the bond matures. Sounds pretty tempting, huh?

Be mindful though, just because bonds are considered safe doesn't mean they're entirely risk-free. Inflation can eat into your returns. Plus if a company goes under, you might not get back the full amount you invested in a corporate bond. It's important to diversify and balance your portfolio to mitigate potential losses.

On a closing note, bonds can serve you best if utilized the right way. They can potentially provide steady income and have benefits of guaranteeing your investment if held to maturity, tax advantages, and act as a safety hedge against the volatility in the stock market.

As with everything in the financial world, don't bet your house on bonds alone. Mix it up. Remember, diversification is the spice of life and certainly the essence of a solid investment portfolio. The whole 'don't put all your eggs in one basket' shebang.

Bottom line: Bonds are a solid option as a source of steady income for your investment portfolio. Understanding them can amplify your savings game in a safe and steady way. Remember, investing isn't just about hitting the jackpot; it's about making consistent, educated decisions that could build your fortune over time.

Mutual Funds

Let's imagine that in front of you are two options for vacationing. Option one: You rent a boat and sail out alone. Option two: You book a trip with a premium cruise liner filled with experienced crew members. In the first case, you're the novice sailor trying to navigate the rough seas of the Pacific Ocean, and in the second, you're relaxing on the deck, cocktail in hand, while a seasoned captain steers you through the choppy waters. That's sort of what it's like to invest in mutual funds.

Mutual funds, as the name suggests, are collective investment vehicles. They pool together money from different investors and use the combined resources to purchase a diversified set of securities - stocks, bonds, and others. This gives individuals the opportunity to invest in a large portfolio of assets, which would be risky or expensive to manage on their own.

Each investor in a mutual fund owns 'units', which represent a portion of the holdings of the fund. This way, even with a smaller amount of investment, you're able to own a diverse array of securities. Broad diversification helps spread out risk - if one company or sector fails, it's only a tiny portion of your overall investment portfolio that takes a hit.

For the beginners out there, mutual funds are a smart place to start your investment journey. It's like having your dollars ride shotgun with a skilled driver who knows the investment roads well. This driver, in reality, is the fund manager. Fund managers are professionals who decide what securities to buy or sell based on extensive research, analysis, and strategy. They're the captains steering your investment ship safely through the turbulent market seas.

Another big plus of mutual funds is liquidity. They can usually be bought or sold on any business day, meaning you'll have relatively quick access to your money if you need it.

Also, mutual funds can be a very cost-effective way of investing. Ever heard of the saying 'economies of scale'? It means that as the size of operation increases, costs per unit decrease. As mutual funds pool together money from so many investors, they're often able to negotiate lower transaction costs. You get to share these cost benefits, awesome, right?

Now, you might be thinking, 'This all sounds great, but what's the catch?' Well, as with any investment, mutual funds come with their own set of risks. The value of a mutual fund depends upon the performance of the securities it decides to buy. So, if these securities do not perform well, the value of the fund might go down. Remember, no investment is risk-free.

And yes, although mutual fund managers are experienced professionals, they're not modern-day Nostradamuses. Despite their knowledge and strategies, they may still make investment decisions that don't pan out as planned, affecting the fund's performance negatively.

There's also a type of mutual fund known as index funds. These funds aim to mimic the performance of a specific index like the S&P 500. The idea is, instead of trying to beat the market, you're trying to replicate its performance. Index funds typically have lower fees since you're not really paying for a manager's skill and expertise.

As you can see, mutual funds can be a potent addition to your investment toolbox, especially if you're not much into managing your investments individually. It's a practical way of putting your money to work without requiring a Wall Street level of expertise or a Scrooge McDuck level of wealth.

But remember, the cruise ship doesn't promise smooth sailing all the time. Be ready for potential storms by doing your homework. Understand the mutual fund prospectus, research the fund manager's performance history, check the fund's fees, and only then, go on for the expedition.

Mutual funds may seem complex, but they're not dark magic. With some time and effort, you can grasp how they work and use them to bolster your financial growth. Remember, in the quest for financial freedom, every investment opportunity counts. Mutual funds are just one of the aspects of the investment universe, so explore, understand, and invest smartly.

Real Estate

Having learned about stocks, bonds, and mutual funds, it's time to delve into another viable investment: real estate. Investing in real estate isn't a new concept. It's a time-tested method that many young individuals are gaining interest in, and rightly so. Major players in the field aren't mega-corporations or Wall Street firms, but regular people who've managed to secure financial freedom by investing smartly.

Real estate is tangible property comprised of land and anything on it, including buildings, flora, and natural resources. When investing in real estate, you're actually buying physical land or property. Some real estate investments can earn you money every month while others appreciate over time for a more significant, long-term gain.

One of the most appealing things about real estate as an investment is its capacity for delivering consistent cash flow. If you end up renting out your property, you could gain income from tenants each month. This steady stream of passive income is an appealing aspect in terms of savings and building wealth but don't underestimate the effort that goes into managing and maintaining your property.

Now you might be thinking, "I'm in my 20s. How can I possibly afford to invest in real estate?" It's a fair question. Most people start by 'house hacking', a term for living in one part of the property and renting out the rest. House hacking allows one to cut down personal living expenses while simultaneously generating income.

Keep in mind though, investing in real estate is not for everyone. It requires patience, dealing with tenants can be challenging, and it's definitely not a quick-get-rich method. Yet, for those prepared to invest time and effort, it can be rewarding in the long run.

Additionally, you must understand that real estate involves housing industry and market trends, which are subject to fluctuations. Property values can rise and fall based on economic factors, interest rates, and market demand. Conducting thorough market research before investing ensures that you make informed decisions and can help prevent financial loss.

Here's another thing: real estate investing isn't restricted to just buying, renting, or selling properties. You could get creative too. You can flip houses—buy a run-down property, renovate it, and sell it at a profit. There's also the possibility of investing in real estate investment trusts (REITs), which allows one to invest in a portfolio of properties without actually owning a physical one.

Investing in a REIT is similar to investing in a stock. REITs are companies that own or finance income-generating real estate, and you can buy shares in these companies. It's a great option for those interested in real estate but not keen on the idea of being a landlord.

Another alternative to conventional real estate investing is "crowdfunded" real estate. This newer approach allows you to invest small amounts of money with other people to buy expensive properties. While this might sound more manageable, remember that it still needs effort and research to ensure you're getting into a good deal.

One advantage of investing in real estate is the tax benefits it presents. Things like depreciation, mortgage interest deductions, and home office deductions can offset income and lower your tax liability. However, it's crucial to consult with a tax professional to understand and maximize these benefits accurately.

Given that real estate is a tangible asset, it can also provide a hedge against inflation. As prices increase over time, so does the value of your real estate investment. This tends to make real estate a safer bet over the long term compared to other types of investments.

In conclusion, real estate can be a fruitful way to get your money working for you, providing both regular income and long-term returns. However, the golden rule is the same as with any other investment - research thoroughly, and don't be hesitant to ask for professional advice. It takes time and patience to become proficient, but keep in mind, the journey toward financial freedom isn't a sprint; it's a marathon.

So there you have it. You're now aware of another lucrative investment vehicle. Real estate, as with any venture, has its ups and downs. However, with careful planning, persistence and due diligence, it can play a critical role in your journey to financial success. Remember, fortunes are slowly built upon the foundation of sound financial decisions you make in your 20s.

Chapter 7: Financial Risks and How to Manage

If you're going to play the game, you've gotta be ready to roll the dice. But here's the deal, it doesn't mean recklessly putting all your chips on one number and closing your eyes in hope. In financial terms, this translates to understanding risk, learning to measure it, and managing it. Now, every sort of investment involves some amount of risk. But it's not necessarily a bad thing. A well-calculated risk can lead to a reward which is profit, growth or both. And that's why we need to talk about how to build a safe financial portfolio. You see, a good portfolio is a mix of different types of investments which balances the risk. And the trick here is diversification. It's like instead of betting everything on one card, you're spreading your bets over multiple rounds to improve your odds. So, one loss doesn't knock you out of the game, it's just a small setback and you're still sitting at the table, ready for the next round.

Risk and Rewards

The world of financial growth revolves around the concepts of risks and rewards. Like every decision in life, making financial decisions means balancing the potential risks against the possible rewards. Let's dive deep into understanding this paradigm.

You've already learned what investing is all about. You know that the money you invest has the potential to generate greater wealth over time. But, it's essential to understand that this process isn't without risk. There's a chance, though, the investment you make can lose its value. That, my friend, is what we call 'risk'.

On the other hand, 'reward' is the potential benefit you could gain from taking on the risk. That might be the accumulation of wealth, an increase in your investment's value, or the generation of dividends or interest. It's the upside of the risk you've taken.

Risk and reward are directly related – the higher the risk of an investment, the higher the potential reward. Conversely, a lower risk generally leads to a lower potential reward. Therefore, your investment strategy should be guided by the amount of risk you're willing to stomach – known as your risk tolerance.

Everyone has a different level of risk tolerance. It's a subjective measure based on your personal comfort level with risk. It's influenced by several factors, including your age, financial goals, and overall financial situation. Younger investors tend to have a higher risk tolerance because they have more time to recover from potential financial losses. However, it's important to never risk more than you're comfortable with.

Your risk tolerance will guide your investment approach. Some folks like to play it safe, purchasing stable, time-tested investments that offer lower risks and rewards. Others prefer to take risks, potentially reaping significant rewards if their bet pays off. There's no right or wrong approach here; it's all about knowing your comfort level with risk.

How do you determine what level of risk is right for you? It all starts with a careful evaluation of your financial situation and goals. If you can handle the potential for loss and you're gunning for high gains, a riskier investment may be a good fit. On the other hand, if you want a more predictable return or can't afford to lose money, a safer investment is a smarter choice.

Keep in mind, investing isn't about making money overnight. It's about making consistent, smart decisions over time and letting the power of compound interest and market gains increase your wealth. Therefore, it's vital to maintain a diverse portfolio so that the risk is spread throughout various investments, and not just concentrated in one.

A useful way to mitigate risk is to diversify your investments. This means spreading your money across different types of investments, like stocks, bonds, and real estate. This strategy can help cushion some of the financial impact if one of your investments takes a hit. As the saying goes—don't put all your eggs in one basket.

Also, make sure you're not investing money that you need for essential expenses. A good rule of thumb is to maintain an emergency fund that covers 3-6 months' worth of living expenses. This money should not be risked in the market; it's your safety net if things don't go according to plan.

One of the most crucial points to understand about risk and reward is that while higher risk can lead to higher rewards, it can also lead to bigger losses. It's important not to be tempted by the promise of big rewards without fully understanding the potential risks.

It's always wise to keep a pulse on your investments, regularly assessing the risk and reward balance. Stay educated, do your research, keep atop market trends, and don't shy away from consulting financial advisors if you're unsure.

Risk-taking in the financial world isn't about being reckless; it's about understanding the landscape and making calculated decisions. It's the key to growing your wealth over time while ensuring that you're not unduly exposing yourself to potential financial catastrophe.

Remember, investing involves risks, including losing hard-earned money. But by understanding the role of risk and reward in investing, defining your risk tolerance, and diversifying your investments, you can navigate the financial seas with confidence and work towards achieving your financial goals.

Building a Safe Financial Portfolio

Now that we've tackled the concept of risk and covered the importance of balancing it, let's dive into the nitty-gritty of building a safe financial portfolio. Remember, a portfolio is essentially the collection of all your investments in one place.

Think of your financial portfolio as a garden. You've got various plants (investments) that need different kinds of care (risk management and monitoring). If you plant a variety of seeds (diversify), the chances of having a blooming garden (financial success) are significantly improved. The whole gardening metaphor isn't just for show; it's a pretty spot-on representation of how to build a safe financial portfolio.

First things first, diversification is key. Yes, you heard that right! Keep your eggs in different baskets. This means if you are investing in stocks, don't just put all your money in tech stocks or healthcare stocks. Spread it out. Same goes for bonds, mutual funds, and real estate too. You don't want all your money tied up in one type of investment.

Diversification isn't just about investing in different sectors though. You also want to think about the size of your investments. In other words, you want a mix of small, mid, and large-cap stocks in your portfolio. Each carries a different risk and potential return, diversifying your portfolio in size and sector can help reduce the overall risk.

Another significant factor to consider when constructing your portfolio is asset allocation. This simply refers to the division of your investments across different asset classes, such as stocks, bonds, real estate, and cash equivalents. The right allocation for you depends on your risk tolerance, financial goals, and investment timeline.

ETFs or Exchange-Traded Funds can also be a reliable option in constructing a diversified portfolio. They are essentially a basket of securities that trade on an exchange, like a stock. They can contain stocks, commodities, or bonds, or a mix of investment types, offering instant diversification in a single trade.

Some investors also take into account macroeconomic and geopolitical factors when building their portfolio. The economy's state, interest rates, political stability, and even factors like climate change can affect investment returns. Being mindful of the bigger picture can help you adjust your portfolio and take advantage of market influences.

The concept of rebalancing is equally crucial for a well-rounded financial portfolio. This is about adjusting your portfolio periodically to maintain your desired level of asset allocation and risk. If a particular investment does exceptionally well and now represents a larger portion of your portfolio than you intended, you may need to sell some of it off. It's all about maintaining balance and staying true to your original strategy.

Your financial portfolio should also consider your tax situation. Certain investment accounts offer tax advantages for saving for specific purposes such as retirement or education. Explore options like IRAs, 401(k)s, and 529 plans to reduce your tax bill and keep more of your money working for you.

Now, all these strategies don't mean that your portfolio will never experience a loss. But what they can do is help minimize the potential loss, and in the investment world, that's a win. Remember, the goal here isn't just to make money but to build lasting, sustainable wealth.

Also, don't forget to keep a close eye on your investments. Regularly review your portfolio to ensure it aligns with your financial goals and adjust if necessary. Your financial goals might change over time, so it's good to reassess your portfolio periodically.

Building a safe financial portfolio may seem daunting at first. But remember, Rome wasn't built in a day. It takes time, patience, knowledge, and regular effort. So, don't rush, take the time to understand each aspect of your portfolio, and make informed decisions.

In the end, the goal is to achieve financial freedom and stability. And it all starts with building a well-diversified and balanced portfolio that fits your financial goals and risk tolerance.

Chapter 8: Building a Solid Credit Score

Navigating the seas of financial independence won't be as smooth if you don't have a good credit score as your compass. You need to understand your credit score—it's not just some random number, it's a reflection of your financial responsibility. Think of it as your adult report card for financial institutions to gauge your creditworthiness. And here's the simple truth: the higher your credit score, the less risk you pose to lenders, which translates into lower interest rates and better loan terms. But how do you build a good credit score? You gotta start by making punctual payments on debts and bills, then ensure that the amount of credit you're utilizing isn't too high compared to your overall credit limit. Steer clear off debts as much as you can, but if you do have any, pay them down promptly. Apply for new credit accounts only as needed but keep the old ones open too for a longer credit history. It's a slow and steady game, but it's worth playing. Making these good habits a part of your financial routine could elevate your credit score, opening better doors in your financial journey. Let's not forget, while having a good credit score is significant, it should not endorse overspending. It's all about balance, pals.

Understanding Your Credit Score

When dealing with the brass tacks of personal finance, you can't ignore the influence of your credit score. This three-digit number carries more weight than you'd ever expect and could be the difference between having a dream house and having just a dream. So, sit back, relax, and let's dive into what a credit score is.

At its simplest, a credit score is a numerical representation of your creditworthiness, or how likely you are to repay a debt. Lenders and creditors use it as a barometer of sorts, assessing how risky it might be to lend you money or provide you with credit.

But what components make up this all-important score? In general, credit scores are calculated using five main factors: your payment history, the amounts owed, the length of your credit history, any new credit you've applied for, and the types of credit you use. Each factor carries a different weight and contributes differently to your overall credit score. For instance, your payment history is the heaviest hitter, forming about 35% of your total score, while new credit accounts only contribute about 10%.

Payment history is how regularly you've made your payments on time. On-time payments will send your credit score soaring, while missed payments take a serious toll. Hence, it's key to set reminders for when bills are due to ensure you don't fall behind.

The amounts owed or credit utilization are another considerable chunk of your credit score pie, clocking in at 30%. Here's how it works: if you're constantly maxing out your credit cards or getting dangerously close to your credit limit, your credit score could plummet. Aim to keep usage under 30% of your total credit limit.

The length of your credit history makes up 15% of your credit score. It considers the age of your oldest account, the average age of all your accounts, and the age of specific account types. Generally speaking, the longer your history—

particularly if it also comes with responsible usage—the better for your credit score.

New credit inquiries account for 10% of your credit score, and this bit can be a little tricky. Simply put, if you apply for too many new lines of credit at once, there may be a negative impact on your score. Lenders could see this rush for credit as a sign of financial trouble, making you seem riskier.

The final 10% comes from the types of credit in use. Having a mix of different types of credit, like installment loans, credit cards, and retail accounts, can mildly boost your credit score. However, this doesn't mean you should run out and open a slew of different credit accounts. Remember the golden rule: only take out credit that you need and can afford.

Your credit score can significantly impact the terms and rates of any credit granted. For instance, a higher credit score usually translates into lower interest rates on loans and credit cards. Meanwhile, a lower credit score can result in higher rates or even outright denial of credit.

Therefore, keeping an eye on your credit score is vital. But how do you do that? Well, a number of companies provide free access to your credit score. Furthermore, many credit card issuers feature free credit score access as a part of their cardholder perks.

It's also crucial to check your credit reports regularly. They provide the information used to calculate your credit score and may contain errors. Spotting errors early and ensuring that your credit report stays accurate will help keep your credit score in good shape.

So, there you have it. Understanding your credit score might feel overwhelming, but in reality, it all comes down to being responsible with your credit, paying your debts on time, and being strategic about how and when you borrow. Start cultivating good habits now, and watch your credit score climb over time.

In the next section, we'll cover some actionable steps to building a good credit score. So, stay with us. Your financial freedom is just around the corner!

Steps to Building a Good Credit Score

Now that we understand a bit about credit scores and their importance, let's dive into creating a high credit score. Building a solid credit score may seem like a daunting task, especially if you're just starting out, but it's more manageable than you think.

The first step to building credit involves understanding your starting point. Get your hands on your credit report. It's free once a year from each of the three major credit bureaus: Experian, Equifax, and TransUnion. Reviewing your credit report can help you identify outstanding debts, late payments, or even errors that may be impacting your credit score.

Next, start by making on-time payments. Remember, payment history makes up to 35% of your FICO score, which is the most commonly used credit scoring model. So, if you have debts, make sure you're paying them on time, every time. This includes everything from loans to utility bills.

Don't worry if you don't have any credit history. You can build some by getting a credit card, but be careful. It's a double-edged sword because while it can aid in building credit, if not handled properly can plunge you into debt. Start off with a secured credit card which is much easier for beginners to get accepted. Just remember to make all your payments on time and never go over your credit limit.

Try to keep your credit card balance below 30% of your available credit limit. This means if your credit limit is $1000, try not to carry a balance of more than $300. This is a part of credit utilization and it makes up 30% of your credit score. Keeping this ratio low shows lenders that you can handle credit responsibly.

Another tip to boost your score is to not close any old credit cards you might have. Length of credit history contributes to 15% of your FICO score. Having a lengthy credit history shows lenders that you have experience handling debt.

Around the same vein, try to build a mix of credit. The FICO score also considers the different types of credit accounts you have. This includes credit cards, student loans, auto loans, and mortgages. Having a mix of these types of accounts can boost your score, but remember, only take out a loan or another credit card if you need it and can afford it.

While you're building your credit, avoid opening too many new credit accounts at once. This can lead to a hard inquiry on your account, which can negatively impact your score. Focus on responsibly managing the credit you already have before looking to expand.

If you happen to find errors on your credit report, don't panic. You have the right to dispute these errors with the credit bureaus. If the bureau agrees with your dispute, they will correct the error on your report, potentially boosting your score.

Lastly, be patient. Building a good credit score doesn't happen overnight. It's a continuous process that requires dedication and responsible money management. Stay committed to your goal, and over time, your credit score will improve.

Building a good credit score isn't rocket science, and even if it seems a bit complex at first, don't sweat it. Start by taking the first step in understanding your credit score and slowly hammering away at it step by step. Always keep in mind, on-time payments, low credit utilization, and a good mix of credit – these are the key factors in building a solid credit score.

Keep this proverb in mind: Slow and steady wins the race. You're playing a long game when you're building your credit score. Rushing can do more harm than good, so stay patient and stay disciplined.

Remember, a good credit score opens many doors and opportunities in the financial world. It's a cornerstone of your financial freedom and a stepping stone to a secure financial future. So lace up your boots, grab the reins, and get that credit score soaring!

Armed with this knowledge, you're ready to tackle the next chapter: ultimately achieving financial independence. It may seem a lofty goal, but it's more achievable than you think. With the right plan and steps, financial freedom is within your reach.

Chapter 9: Financial Independence and Retiring Young

Now that we've mapped the jungle that is credit, let's press on to the promised land: Financial Independence and Retiring Young. So, what's this financial independence thing all about? Well, it's the ultimate level of financial freedom where your assets generate enough income to cover your expenses with no need for employment or receiving financial assistance. Center stage are your investments - ya know, the stocks, bonds, mutual funds, and real estate we've touched on already - working overtime so you don't have to. Retirement might seem like a million miles away, but trust me, acting now will fast track you to your dream early retirement. The method to this madness is remarkably straightforward: saving aggressively and investing wisely. Trading your designer sneakers, lattes, and luxury vacations now could mean swapping them for endless beach days, globetrotting, or simply untroubled living later on. With the right investment strategy tailored to your financial situation and risk tolerance, the fruits of your efforts can amass to a fortune that frees you from the workforce way sooner than your peers. Instead of imagining, start living the dream of Financial Independence and Retiring Young.

What is Financial Independence?

Imagine a life where you're not constantly worrying about making ends meet, paying off debts, or working a job you hate just so you can pay the bills. Sounds awesome right? That's essentially what financial independence is all about. It's the freedom to make choices that are not influenced by financial constraints. It's about striking a balance between income and expenses, and having choices about work and how you spend your time.

Many people think financial independence is tied to an age, like retirement. But more accurately, it's tied to your resources and expenses. It's about reaching a point in life where your assets (like investments, savings, or properties) can comfortably cover your living expenses, without relying on a regular paycheck.

Why does financial independence matter, particularly for young people? The answer is simple: freedom, control, and peace of mind. Achieving financial independence gives you the liberty to choose the lifestyle you want. Perhaps you want to travel the world, start a family, or even pursue a passion project - that's all possible when you're financially independent.

Let's clarify something important, though. Financial independence doesn't mean being fabulously wealthy. It's not about owning multiple homes or sports cars. Rather, it's about having enough passive income to cover your expenses. It's about achieving a state where you don't feel financially strained, stressed, or vulnerable.

Perhaps you're wondering, "Do I need millions to be financially independent?" Not necessarily. Really, it's about your expenses being lower than your income, particularly your passive income (money you make without actively working). If you can achieve that, you're financially independent.

Now, let's break down the concept of financial independence a bit further. There are generally four stages. The first stage is financial dependence, where you rely on someone else, perhaps your parents, for financial support. The next stage is financial solvency, where you can meet your financial commitments but you may still carry some debt.

The third stage is financial stability. At this point, you have an emergency fund saved up and you're able to live comfortably. However, you're not yet financially free because you still need your active income (usually from a job) to cover your living expenses.

The last stage is the biggie! Financial independence. This is where your passive income can completely cover your expenses. Note that at this stage, working becomes optional. You could decide to retire early, change careers, or focus on other things that matter to you.

Reaching financial independence can seem like a daunting task, especially if you're wondering how you're supposed to save and invest while also enjoying your youth. That's a valid concern. However, it's important to remember that financial independence isn't about denying yourself all pleasures. It's about spending wisely, investing smartly, and making your money work for you. It's about finding a balance that allows you to enjoy today, while also preparing for tomorrow.

Wrap your head around this: it's not so much how much you earn that leads you to financial independence, but rather how much you save and invest. In other words, even on a moderate income, by being smart with your money, you can still achieve financial independence.

Oh, and you should also know there is no single path to achieving financial independence. We all have different income levels, expenses, lifestyles, and financial goals. It's critical to figure out a strategy that works best for you and aligns with your personal values and goals.

Achieving financial independence might necessitate changes in various aspects of your life. You might need to adjust your lifestyle, spending habits, and savings rate. Maybe you'll need to learn more about investments and how to generate passive income. It's a journey, so buckle down, keep learning, and stay disciplined.

Finally, keep in mind, financial independence is not an end itself. It's a means to an end. It provides the foundation for you to lead the kind of life you envision for yourself and those you care about. It's not about the destination, but the freedom and resources it gives you to enjoy the ride. So, cheers to the journey to financial independence. It's entirely possible, and it starts with one small step.

How to Reach Financial Independence

Reaching financial independence is no small feat, but the journey needs methodical planning and disciplined execution. Don't worry, you aren't alone in this journey. Let's chart out a step-by-step guide to work towards this interesting but achievable goal.

Firstly, understand what financial independence means for you. It's different for everyone. For some, it might mean not having to work again, for others, it might mean being able to pursue a passion without worrying about the paycheck. So, the first step is defining what financial independence means to you personally.

Next, you need to know your 'why.' Why do you want to achieve financial independence? Is it to secure a comfortable retirement, to travel around the world, or to invest in your passion projects? Your 'why' can act as a driving force when the road to financial independence seems tough.

The third step is assessing your current financial state. Recollect everything we've discussed so far like understanding your income, expenses, debt, and investments. Evaluate your financial health meticulously. This will help you judge how far you are from your goal.

Setting those long-term financial goals comes next. Based on your assessment, decide on your money milestones. Whether it's buying a house, or saving enough to live comfortably for 20 years without work, be clear and precise.

Maintaining a strict budget is integral to this process. By now, you should already be practicing this from our previous sessions. If not, it's never too late to start. Remember, every penny saved is a step closer to your independence.

Next, reduce your debts. Try to eliminate high-interest debt first and make a plan to pay off the remaining in a systematic manner. Debt can be a serious impediment in your journey towards financial freedom, and you need to tackle it head-on.

Remember, saving is just one part of the process, make your money work for you. Investment is the key. Mutual funds, stocks, bonds, real estate, select your avenues wisely and diversify. Hold on to your patience because the success of most investments can't be seen overnight.

Ensuring that you've got an emergency fund is extremely important. Financial shocks can throw the best laid plans off track. An emergency fund acts as a buffer, ensuring you don't fall off the wagon on your way to financial independence.

Understanding and managing financial risks are also critical. Remember that every investment carries a certain level of risk. Therefore, diversifying your portfolio across different assets can help you manage these risks effectively.

Also, don't forget the power of compound interest. The sooner you start investing, the more time your money has to grow. Compounding interest can make a huge difference in your investments over time.

Don't overlook the importance of a good credit score. It can open up better financial avenues for you. Deftly managing credit and ensuring timely repayments can keep up your score.

Lastly, but most importantly, make financial education an ongoing journey. Stay updated about the latest trends in the financial world, seek advice from experts, learn from the financial journeys of others, and continually adapt and tweak your plan with the changing markets.

Reaching financial independence won't happen overnight, and it's not always an easy path. It demands patience, discipline, amendments to your lifestyle, and sometimes, your mindset. But remember, the journey is just as important as the destination. Each step you take towards financial independence not only brings financial rewards but also makes you more knowledgeable and in control of your life.

Start your journey towards financial independence today—it's never too early. Your future self will thank you for your smart and timely decisions.

Chapter 10: Case Studies

Building upon all the financial wisdom and guidelines we've laid out so far, in this chapter, we'll dive into some real-life case studies to give you a clearer picture of how all these tips and strategies play out in practical scenarios. We're going to tell you about three different young folks, who just like you, were eager to lay a strong financial groundwork for their future. At 20 something, they too faced their share of financial hurdles, made some mistakes but eventually triumphed over them. Through their journeys, you'll learn how they budgeted, invested, and managed their finances to become financially independent early. Hopefully, their actions, decisions, and outcomes will give you some useful insights, and more importantly, the confidence that you too can attain financial freedom. Stay tuned, my young savant, truths of the financial world await you!

Case Study 1

Let's dive into our first case study, featuring Mike, a fresh-faced graduate working his first job out of college. His annual salary is roughly $50,000, with some variable income from freelance projects. Despite finding success at an early age, Mike knows that he can't take his foot off the gas. He's committed to setting himself up for the future, and he understands that the right mindset and strategies can turn this initial success into long-term financial security.

With a smart understanding of his finances, Mike quickly learns the value of starting early. He knows that his age and income level make him a perfect candidate for harnessing the power of compound interest. One can indeed argue that the 'eighth wonder of the world' is on his side. Every dime he saves now will be worth much more in the future, thanks to the magic of compound interest.

Part of Mike's financial strategy is setting clear, achievable goals. He outlines his short-term and long-term financial aims, understanding that setting those goals now will help him achieve financial independence in the future. Some of his short-term goals include paying off student loans and purchasing a reliable vehicle, while his long-term goal is owning property without the bane of mortgage payments.

To make these goals a reality, Mike sets a strict yet realistic budget and sticks to it passionately. He tracks his income and expenses meticulously and disciplines himself to spend within his means, making sure not to shortchange his savings. Budgeting allows him to live comfortably without living paycheck to paycheck, a crucial aspect in his pursuit of financial freedom.

Mike is intelligent with his debts too. He strikes a balance and understands the difference between good and bad debt. The student loans, for example, are an investment he made in his education and although he's keen on paying them off quickly, he doesn't view them negatively. However, he opts against any unnecessary credit card debt or high-interest personal loans that don't contribute to his wealth-building goals.

Mike employs various saving strategies, focusing heavily on building an emergency fund. He realizes the importance of financial cushions that can alleviate unexpected life events. He also uses a saving account to stash some cash away consistently while utilizing automatic saving features to minimize the temptation of spending impulsively.

One of Mike's most proactive strategies is investing. He recognizes the strength of diversifying his portfolio, dabbling in stocks, bonds, mutual funds, and even real estate. With a bit of research and the knack to take calculated risks, Mike builds an impressive portfolio. He places particular emphasis on investing in index funds as they often provide are a stable, low-cost form of mutual funds.

Throughout his financial journey, Mike always keeps in mind the balance between risk and reward in his investments. Assessing financial risk is perhaps the trickiest part of his endeavor, yet it's also the one where he learns the most. Mike assembles a safe, well-balanced financial portfolio guided by his tolerance to risk and financial objectives.

Simultaneously, Mike is proactive about building a robust credit score, realizing that a good score will offer better borrowing rates and enhance his financial opportunities. He's consistent with his credit card payments, keeps his credit utilization rate low, and refrains from applying for unnecessary credit.

Through diligent saving, smart investing, and avoidance of detrimental debt, Mike is on the path to financial independence. He's setting his own rules, making money work for him rather than him working for money. Mike may not consider retiring young yet, but he certainly enjoys the privilege of choice, thanks to his careful financial planning and actions.

This case study serves as an applicable example for everyone in their 20s to follow. Mike's financial strategies aren't anything out of the ordinary, they revolve around discipline, responsibility, and being proactive. If you can grasp and apply these strategies, you're positioning yourself for a financially secure future, just like Mike.

Case Study 2

Meet Eric. Eric was a typical twenty-something college graduate, hustling to pay off his student loan debt. He had a stable job in a good market sector, earning roughly the average income for his age and field. He had some ideas about savings and investments but, like many young adults, he needed guidance to put those ideas into a solid plan.

Eric was not a stranger to money management. Coming from a humble background, he had always been conscious about expenses. However, his initial struggles weren't aimed at wealth accumulation, but survival. So, when he first started earning, he could barely manage to balance his debts and monthly bills, let alone think about savings or investments. He knew the importance of starting young but didn't have a clear guide on the practical steps to take.

One day, he was introduced to this idea of financial freedom and retiring young. Intrigued and determined, Eric decided to embark on a journey of smart money management to achieve his newfound financial goals. To start off, he created a realistic budget that allowed him to cover all of his essential bills and commitments, and included a small allowance for enjoyment, because after all, life isn't just about sacrificing, is it?

Eric soon made a critical change in saving instead of spending. Every month, he set aside a fixed percentage of his salary. This method of saving is called 'Paying Yourself First.' Despite having student loans to repay, he prioritized saving. This helped him build an emergency fund, which, he realized, could provide a safety net against sudden unemployment or unexpected expenses. Something he didn't have before.

Eric then turned his focus towards balancing and managing his debts. He started by distinguishing between 'good' and 'bad' debt. He realized that while his student loan was considered as 'good' debt (as it invested in his own professional growth), the credit card balance he carried every month fell into the 'bad' debt category. With this understanding, he worked out a plan to pay off his 'bad' debt first and then handle the 'good' ones.

His next step was setting short-term and long-term financial goals. Eric's short-term goal was to eliminate credit card debt completely. Doggedly focused, he achieved this in under a year. His long-term goal, on the other hand, was to fully pay off his student loan in five years. While this sounded ambitious at first, sticking to his budget helped Eric stay on track.

Now that Eric had a handle on his debts and savings, he began to explore investing. He started small in the stock market, buying shares from companies he believed in and understood. This gave him a practical foundation in a complex field. Still part of his long-term strategy, Eric also decided to further diversify his portfolio by investing in low-cost index funds and mutual funds.

Real estate investments had always been Eric's dream, but this goal seemed too huge to be achievable in the immediate future. However, he decided to include this as a part of his long term plans. His strategy? To buy rental properties and have the rent cover the mortgages while potentially appreciating in value.

With a growing investment portfolio, Eric knew he had to also manage the associated risks. He diversified his investments across stocks, mutual funds, and planned real estate investments. This way, he wasn't placing all his eggs in one basket and secured varying degrees of risk and return.

Eric was on the perfect track to financial freedom. However, there was one more key area he decided to monitor closely—his credit score. With regular check-ups and smart credit handling, Eric began building a stellar credit score. He knew that a good credit score could prove extremely beneficial, providing favorable loan rates for his future real estate investments.

Eric's story stands as an example of how ordinary individuals can turn their economic lives around right from their twenties. Starting from balancing his most basic expenses to stepping into the realm of investments, Eric successfully paved his way towards financial independence. His journey, albeit filled with challenges, illuminated the path for achieving financial freedom with focused planning, disciplined saving, and wise investing.

At the end of five years, Eric was not just free of his student loan, but he was also a proud owner of two small rental properties, a healthy stock portfolio, and an excellent credit score. Sure, he enjoyed his fair share of relaxation and entertainment, but he also made sure to invest in his financial future.

Preparation, determination, and consistency were his secret ingredients. This case study aims to prove that financial independence is not a myth, but a real possibility if one starts early, saves regularly, makes wise investment decisions, and maintains a good credit standing. If Eric could do it on an average income, so can you!

Case Study 3

Let's jump right into another scenario illustrating the principles we've been discussing throughout this book. You're about to meet Jane, a 28-year-old lawyer with a hefty student loan debt.

When Jane finished law school, she owed $100,000 in student loan debt. Her initial salary was $60,000 per year. At first glance, you might think that she was in over her head. But was she really? Let's dig into the numbers and see the financial steps Jane took to turn it around.

Upon starting her career, Jane began setting aside a fixed percentage of her income for her savings, retirement account, and investments. She didn't allow her student loan debt to scare her away from saving money, rather she used this motivation to aggressively save and invest.

Even though she had the monstrous student loan, Jane began by creating a budget. A large chunk of her income was going towards the student loan repayment, but Jane made sure to squeeze in a savings component into her budget too. This discipline allowed her to ensure that she was not just paying off her duties but was also adding to her wealth.

Jane then decided to start small, investing 10% of her yearly income towards a mix of stocks, bonds and mutual funds. She understood the risks associated with investing, but she also kept in mind the potential rewards. She diversified her investments wisely to lower the risks.

The goal was clear for her: achieve financial independence. Jane wasn't phased by the fancy lifestyle that most of her colleagues enjoyed. Instead, she lived a modest lifestyle focusing on her long-term financial goals.

She stuck firmly to her budget, cutting down on unnecessary luxuries and expenses. Jane was a great example of someone who understood the value of money and didn't let her desires control her finances.

What really made Jane's case inspiring though, was the steps she took to manage her debt. She made her payments on time, never missing a deadline. As a result, her credit score remained healthy throughout this time. Moreover, she created an emergency fund specifically for situations where she might face difficulty in making her loan payments.

Her consistent investments in a diverse portfolio started yielding results in 7-8 years. She continually reinvested her earnings to tap into the power of compound interest. After 10 years, Jane managed to pay off her student loan completely, and her investment portfolio had grown significantly, thanks to her diligent savings and disciplined investing.

Now, Jane has a healthy retirement fund and is financially independent. She no longer worries about surviving paycheck to paycheck, and she's beaten the odds of student loan crisis with her smart financial choices.

But what's special about Jane? Is she a financial genius? Far from it. Jane is just a regular person like you and me. She embraced the power of budgeting, the potential of investing, and the principle of saving to triumph over her financial situation.

It's not about earning a lot of money, it's all about managing money in a smart way. Jane's case illustrates the potential of starting young, the power of compound interest, the advantage of saving, the wonders of investing and smart debt management.

Remember, you could be the next Jane. Your 20s is the time to turn things around. Learn from Jane's story and use these lessons to make smart decisions about your money. Financial independence isn't out of your reach!

In conclusion, Jane's story is a shining example of how understanding your personal finances, diligent saving, smart investing, proper debt management, and sticking to your financial goals can lead to financial freedom, regardless of how daunting your financial situation may initially appear. Take inspiration and initiate your financial journey today.

Conclusion

So, you've made it to the end of this financial journey. From the outset, you've learnt the importance of understanding money and breaking the psychological barriers that pose as roadblocks to saving. You've started young, exploited the power of compound interest and set short-term and long-term financial goals.

With the help of the budgeting basics, you've managed to create not just a budget, but also a roadmap that you've stuck too. Consequently, managing debt didn't seem that uphill a task anymore. You've delayered good and bad debt, taken steps to balance debts and successfully formulated saving strategies which comprise a mix of emergency funds, saving accounts and automatic saving.

Once that was in place, you delved into investing – in stocks, bonds, mutual funds, and real estate. You learned the essentials to manage financial risks, understanding the relationship between risk and rewards. Then, you built a solid, safe financial portfolio that will carry you through any trials and tribulations.

Your credit score isn't something obscure anymore. You've understood how it works and have taken active steps to build a good credit score. You're ready to take the leap towards financial independence and the possibility of an early retirement doesn't seem so outlandish anymore. Success stories from around the globe gave you inspiration and insights for your own journey.

Financial pitfalls are something we've strongly focused on avoiding. Falling into a financial setback is an easy thing to do, but climbing out can be overwhelming. These pitfalls, often unseen, are mostly the result of little to no planning, impulsive shopping, overuse of credit, not saving enough, poor investing and lack of emergency funds. Remembering these will help you safeguard your hard-earned cash.

However, creating a successful financial roadmap takes more than just awareness. It requires you to revisit your plans frequently, to ensure you're on the right track. It's about being adaptable when needed and having the grit to stick to your plan.

Work on your mindset towards money. Remember that it's a tool that can provide security, open opportunities and offer a safety net. Your attitude towards money and wealth, and the mindset with which you approach saving, investing, and spending, can make a world of difference.

Always keep your financial goals in sight and let them be your guiding star in every financial decision you make. Whether these are short-term goals like saving for a vacation or long-term ones like retirement, your goals will help you allocate resources wisely.

Remember, it's never too late to learn and implement a new strategy or approach in your financial journey. Whether it's in understanding the nuances of the stock market, or mastering the art of balance in debt management – every bit counts.

Moreover, although it's crucial to start young due to the awesome power of compound interest, bear in mind that it's never too late to start. Even if you're out of your 20s or even 30s, you can still set financial goals and work towards achieving them systematically with the right approach and determination.

In the end, remember the ultimate goal isn't just about retiring young. It's about attaining financial independence and having the freedom to make choices that aren't dictated by financial limitations. The ability to live not on your own terms, but on the terms set by your dreams and not your bills, that is financial freedom.

Congratulations on completing the first step on this continuous journey of financial enlightenment. Your roadmap to financial freedom is clearer now, and the tools to navigate the terrain are in your hands. Now all you got to do is take the wheel and begin the exciting journey towards financial stability and freedom. Here's to all the best in your financial journey ahead!

Common Financial Pitfalls to Avoid

Laying your financial foundation in your 20s is a powerful move, but it can easily crumble if you're not aware of the hazards. Here's a list of common financial pitfalls you'll want to avoid on your journey to financial freedom.

Misunderstanding Debt: It's easy to fall into the trap of believing all debt is bad. However, there's a difference between good debt and bad debt. Good debt stimulates growth, like an affordable mortgage or a student loan, while bad debt hinders your financial progress. These are usually the result of impulsive purchases on credit cards or high-interest loans.

Not Setting a Budget: As we discussed in the Budgeting Basics chapter, a good budget is quintessential to financial freedom. Without a budget, you're essentially navigating without a map, making it easy to fall off the path.

Lack of Emergency Fund: Life has a way of throwing curveballs—in terms of unexpected expenses—that can sideline even the best-laid financial plans. Always maintain an emergency fund, which can prove to be a lifesaver when faced with unexpected financial downturns. Ignoring this strategy might lead you into unnecessary debt.

Living Paycheck-to-Paycheck: This approach might meet your needs for now, but it isn't sustainable in the long run. It leaves little room for savings and emergency funds, making you more vulnerable to financial crises. Aim to save and invest a part of your income, no matter how small.

Poor Investment Choices: As exciting as investing may be, jumping into it without understanding the risks and rewards can lead to significant losses. Study the market, consult with an advisor, and make informed decisions when choosing stocks, bonds, mutual funds, or real estate.

Not Considering Retirement: Retirement may seem far away in your twenties, but the earlier you start planning, the better. Setting retirement goals and working towards them from a young age puts you in a strong financial position later in life.

Ignoring Credit Score: Your credit score impacts your borrowing capacity and interest rates. Ignoring it can hurt your chances when applying for loans or new credit. Regularly check your credit report for errors and work on improving your score.

Spending more than you earn: This seems like a no-brainer, but it's surprisingly easy to fall into this habit, especially when you have access to credit. Overspending increases debt and decreases saving potential, both of which hinder your path to financial freedom.

Avoiding Professional Help: If the roadmap to financial freedom seems too overwhelming, it's okay to seek professional help. Ignoring the need for a financial advisor because you think it's unnecessary or too expensive could be a costly mistake in the long run.

Skimping on Insurance: In an attempt to save money, one might overlook the importance of a good insurance policy. However, the cost of unforeseen events without insurance is much higher. Whether it's health insurance, rental insurance, or auto insurance, it's essential to be covered.

No Regular Financial Check-ins: Your financial situation will continuously change due to varying factors. Therefore, regular check-ins and adjustments are essential. Financial neglect can lead to unnecessary losses and missed opportunities.

Impulse Buying: Baumol's cost disease theory in economics explains that some costs rise disproportionately compared to others, and this might cause artificial inflation perception. Therefore, mindless spending without understanding this concept might lead to unnecessary debt.

Not diversifying your investments: Putting all your eggs in one basket might seem rewarding initially, but it comes with significant risks. Diversifying your investments can lead to more steady and reliable returns.

Following the Herd: Just because your friends or the majority are investing or spending in certain ways, doesn't mean it's the best choice for your financial situation. Be mindful of your decisions and avoid following the crowd blindly.

Now that we've covered the common financial pitfalls to avoid, you're better equipped to navigate your financial journey, confidently making sound decisions to reach financial freedom. The next section will essentially tie all the chapters together, providing you with a recap and your personal financial roadmap.

Recap and Your Financial Roadmap

Now that we've covered a variety of financial topics, let's review and combine all that knowledge into a significant roadmap for your financial future.

Recall, at our starting point, the value of understanding money and overcoming the psychological barriers to saving. Simply put, the more you know about how wealth works, the easier it becomes to save and grow it. Don't let old beliefs hold you back from making smart financial choices.

The next stop on the journey was recognizing the power of starting young. We explored the magic of compound interest, explaining how it is not the amount of money but the length of time that really makes a difference. So don't wait to plant the financial seeds - the earlier, the better.

We then climbed the mountain of setting financial goals - breaking them down into short-term, long-term, and retirement milestones. Remember to keep your goals SMART, that is, Specific, Measurable, Achievable, Relevant, and Time-bound. And when it comes to retirement, think about how you want to live your golden years and plan accordingly.

Down the path, we dove into the concept of budgets and managing debts. Knowing where your money goes is the first step to taking control of your finances. And when it comes to debt, understand the difference between good and bad debt and learn how to manage it effectively.

After that, we discussed the role of saving strategies, highlighting the importance of emergency funds, saving accounts, and automatic savings. These tactics are your safety nets for unforeseeables, stepping stones to bigger financial goals, and tools to make the act of saving stress-free.

Moving further along your journey, we ventured into the intriguing world of investing. You got a taste of different investment routes like stocks, bonds, mutual funds, and real estate. Don't forget, investing is about diversifying - so consider a mix of these for a balanced portfolio.

We then warned you of the potential risks along your financial journey. Every investment carries some measure of risk, but remember that calculated risks come with rewards. Build a financial portfolio that aligns with your comfort level of risk.

The expedition included a layover at the crossroads of credit score. Understanding your credit score and working to build it up not only gives you leverage when borrowing money but also opens up cheaper financial opportunities.

And our ultimate destination? Financial independence. It's that glorious place where you are not tied to a job for money, instead, your money is working for you. Don't view this as a dream, view it as a goal—an achievable goal if you follow the roadmap.

A practical demonstration of this roadmap was brought to life with case studies. Real-life scenarios help you understand the path better and recognize potential hiccups along the way. They are the perfect examples of what's possible.

Lastly, remember to navigate around common financial pitfalls. Mistakes are bound to happen but you've got a roadmap now, loaded with knowledge from this book. Use it wisely and make adjustments as per your specific needs.

In conclusion, never forget: money management is a marathon, not a spring - the key to financial freedom lies in consistent and smart choices. Keep evolving your financial roadmap as you grow and your needs, goals, and circumstances change. So here's to your financial success, and an exciting, rewarding journey ahead!